The Race for Work
Escape Automation, Transform Your Career and Thrive in the Second Machine Age

Bhoopathi Rapolu

Copyright

Copyright © 2016 by Bhoopathi Rapolu

All rights reserved.

Contents

Copyright ii
Download the Bonuses Free! v
Introduction 1

Section 1: Your Job is More at Risk Than You Think 9
Chapter 1. Productivity Is for Robots 11
Chapter 2. Abundance at the Cost of Jobs 35
Chapter 3. Capitalism Got Disrupted 43
Chapter 4. An Entrepreneur Wants to Change the World 65
Chapter 5. Millennials Redefine Work 75

Section 2: The Sexiest Jobs of the 21st Century 87
Chapter 6. Technologies on the Second Half of the Chess Board .. 89
Chapter 7. The Big Three Technologies 99
Chapter 8. You Are Not an Outsider to the Party 119
Chapter 9. Winning the Race against Machines 127
Chapter 10. The Sexiest Jobs of the 21st Century 141

Section 3: Cracking the Code of the Dream Job 155
Chapter 11. Finding Your Path to Freedom 157
Chapter 12. Dream Job Principles for the 21st Century 169
Chapter 13. The Definitive Roadmap to Your Dream Job 181
Chapter 14. Living with a Dream Job and Beyond 209
Conclusion 221
Acknowledgements 225
About the Author 227
Notes 229

Download the Bonuses Free!

Thank you for buying the book. To get access to all the free resources listed below, please visit http://www.bhoopathi.com/r4w

- Just to say thanks for buying my book, I would like to give you the Audiobook version 100% FREE!
- Bhoopathi's 25+ must-read business books to fuel your dream career. (I keep adding more to this list)
- 10 tools and templates to save you hundreds of hours when finding your dream job and being a top performer at your dream job.
- A Ninety-Day goal setting template to translate the book into actionable steps
- Access to a private community to discuss the book and get support from a community of like-minded individuals to inspire, motivate, and assist each other.

Introduction

"When you cease to dream, you cease to live."
— Malcolm Forbes

In 2012, I was going through the toughest time in my career. In fact, the trouble had actually been brewing for more than 5 years before that. While my friends and family saw me as enjoying a successful job in one of the most respected IT companies in the world, I started feeling like a failure. Towards the end of 2012, I was increasingly fighting a losing battle every day, due to lack of growth, learning, and meaning in what I was doing and, above all, no visible hope for getting out of the mess I was in.

During the same time, with the onslaught of revolutionary technologies such as social media, mobile devices, big data analytics, and cloud computing, there was disruption in many industries. There was certainly no dearth of new technologies in the market. I started hearing about technologies such as IoT, AI and 3D printing, but I had no clue about how to find a job in any of those technologies. These disruptive technologies were rapidly changing the face of both IT and brick-and-mortar industries, creating many opportunities for those clever enough to grab them.

I noticed a slow and dreadful trend (not only in the IT industry but also in many other industries, as well) that is impacting many people who are oblivious of these disruptive technologies. Software is not only eliminating millions of traditional jobs, but also making many earlier software technologies irrelevant, leading to a slow death of careers for those who work with sunset technologies and in obsolete organizational operations.

A fast-growing technology trend is like a major tide in the ocean. If you are part of it, you will move along with it at the same speed at which it is moving forward. Imagine growing your career at the speed of a growing technology or industry. You will see heights in your career beyond your present imagination, but the question is, how can you get into this speed boat? How can you get into a fast-growing technology that can offer you a dream job with more money, meaningful work, and the freedom to do what you love?

This book is about my journey to my dream job and how I have helped others with various unrelated backgrounds to secure their dream jobs in technologies that are growing exponentially. In a concise and easy-to-read manner, *Race for Work* has been designed to help you: 1) systematically assess the risk in your current job; 2) understand how automation is engulfing your career prospects; 3) understand the job opportunities in disruptive technologies; and 4) tell you how to attain your dream job with the proven method that is described in this book.

How It Worked for Me

In June 2013, I secured my dream job in one of these technologies, despite having a seemingly irrelevant background and experience. It was indeed a dream come true, where I suddenly realized the bliss of doing what I love, with greater money and freedom in hand.

We are all self-constrained by our limiting beliefs that our education, experience and limited personal network will not help us get into our dream jobs. In this book, you will find thoroughly tested practical methods and tools to overcome your limiting beliefs and ways to embrace the rushing tide of change to carry you forward in your career.

I have invested thousands of dollars in some of the elite courses that teach one how to crack this puzzle of getting into a dream job. I have also read hundreds of bestselling books and top-rated articles on these subjects (career, technology and networking), and tested the ideas in the real world. However, my experience was not complete until I took over the other side of the game: I became a recruiter in a fast-growing technology.

I was fortunate enough to be an intrapreneur within my corporate job, in which I built a new business based on big data analytics. In the first 18 months of my dream job, I have shared my experience by speaking at leading business conferences and universities in more than 20 cities across the world. I have also coached more than 100 CEOs and business heads across the world on how to build a business in disruptive technologies and recruit talent. When a new technology enters into a commercial market, nobody has decades of experience to take on senior positions, but that does not stop people from taking enviable positions and driving the market, leading from the front. Millions of people have already found their dream jobs in next-generation technologies and are growing as those technologies grow.

The New Technologies

Though disruptive technologies find their application in one or two industries to begin with, they influence other industries like a wildfire, creating opportunities for those who are ready to grab them. Ignoring them in your industry is like ignoring a high-speed train to your final destination.

Big Data Analytics and Artificial Intelligence (AI) initially found their application in retail, Customer Relationship Management

(CRM) and financial services. However, they have caught up and used in other, totally unrelated industries, such as health care, manufacturing, transportation, etc. They created jobs—not just for data scientists, but for a whole lot of people with a variety of skills and experience, such as business analysts, domain experts, and in fields such marketing, sales, HR, etc.

The Internet of Things (IoT) initially began to be used in industrial applications, but quickly spread to consumer applications. Leading industry analyst firms and companies forecast a trillion-dollar market for IoT. (You heard that right: it was "trillion," with a "T".) Cisco reports that, to realize the promise of IoT, businesses will spend up to $20 trillion by 2020[1]. That is more than the size of the entire US GDP in 2015. Almost no industry is spared from this revolution. Imagine the job opportunities it is going to create and the speed at which it can elevate the careers of the people who can drive this transformation!

3D printing is another such disruption waiting to engulf the market. 3D printing is not just for manufacturing material goods, but also for creating food, human body parts, and whole lot of things we see in our everyday life. With most of our daily goods being 3D-printable, in the next 20 years the world will be significantly different than how it is today.

The Opportunities Are There for Those Who Apply These Methods

For all of those who have a job today, these technologies offer a lifetime of career opportunities in which one can find more meaningful work, money and freedom. This book shows you how to identify the right opportunity for you and how to grab it—usually in not more than 6 months, if you diligently follow the step-by-step method I lay out for you in the later chapters. Before I wrote this book, I had advised and guided hundreds of people from various industries who sent me their rave reviews after they successfully got into their dream jobs.

"With your guidance, I have developed enormous confidence to reach up to great heights. The assignments that you have provided and expert guidance for the approach are still helping me to learn technologies that I initially thought impossible for me. I could carry out current accomplishments at ease. Everything you taught me is helping me to reach my desired goal in life.

Recently I received a star award for my work in my new company. I felt very happy and remembered you at that moment, as without your excellent guidance, I wouldn't have gotten this.

I would like to thank from bottom of my heart. I am very grateful for all you have done for me.

Thank you,
Hari"

"Working in the infrastructure industry for almost 4 years made my life quite monotonous and at some point quite stereotyped. I was fortunate enough to get you as my mentor. The way you transformed my subconscious thoughts into constructive goals is a part that is worth mentioning.

During our first interaction, you told me, 'Identify your problems but give your power and energy to solutions.' These were the lines which put an indelible mark in my thought process.

You helped me realize the fact that I need to take responsibility for all my problems and act on them. You helped me [to look inside myself] and find the answers to my own problems.

We had plenty of interaction thereafter and shared all sorts of problems which I faced. The best part of you is that you are the best listener I have ever met. Your composure made me feel your empathy towards my problem.

I don't remember how many times I re-modified my CV and resent it to you and waited eagerly for your comments. We discussed each point thoroughly. The best part was your way of making me answer for myself. Finally, the day came when I got an 'Okay' signal from you on my CV. It was not much later that my CV got shortlisted for one of the big 4 consulting companies. Before going to the interview, I had clarity on each and every point, as you had made me answerable on each point, which helped me overcome all the hurdles and I got placed in that coveted company.

I think the journey would have never been so beautiful if I had not got you as a mentor. Thank you, sir. Thank you for everything,

Arin

Many people do not attempt to go after their dream jobs not because they don't know about those jobs, but they think they are not the right people for such jobs. In this book, I provide easy-to-follow steps for what you can do to get into your dream job with your *current* skills and experience. You will be better able to understand your strengths and know how to fill any gaps, so that you are ready to face the job market with all the confidence you need to succeed in your quest.

The Time to Act Is Now

The three key elements of a dream job are: 1) meaningful work, 2) more money, and 3) freedom to do what you love. That's why that kind of job is by far the most sought-after thing in the life of any working professional. Achieving it is like having a dream come true. If you are committed to resolving your lifetime career challenge, I am fully confident that this book can help you achieve your goal.

The current technological revolution is an irreversible force that no individual, society, nation or even the whole world can stop. Its single direction is towards greater automation—pumping more and more intelligence into machines, in order to relieve humans from doing the work. When I say machine, it is not necessarily a physical object but can also be a software that can work silently and may be even remotely.

It looks quite positive and optimistic at the outset, but it isn't really good news for those individuals who are currently doing the work that machines are going to appropriate.

The impending danger is going to happen much sooner than you think. It's not just going to affect manual work; even the majority of skilled service work is going to be taken up by machines. You need to understand the threat to your job today and create your escape plan for developing a lifelong employment opportunity. Don't be the person who misses out on the opportunities and then repents when the golden moment has passed. Be the kind of person that other people see and say, "I don't know how you did that. It's really amazing!" To become that person, you need to act now!

The insights you are going to gain from reading this book have already motivated and guided thousands of people to find their dream jobs in disruptive technologies. The practical methods and tools in this book have been proven to create positive and long-lasting results. This is a system which has already been used by thousands of people to define what they love to do, find where such work is available, win interviews, successfully negotiate for more money, and earn their freedom. To achieve your goal, all you need to do is to have faith in the system and follow each step with utmost commitment. You can do this! Take control of your life right now, make it successful, and enjoy the new life you are creating.

Section 1
YOUR JOB IS MORE AT RISK THAN YOU THINK

Chapter 1. Productivity Is for Robots

"Work saves a man from three great evils: boredom, vice, and need." — Voltaire

If I ask you "Who are you?" you most probably will answer the question with what you do for a living. We commonly identify ourselves with our contribution to society in terms of a clearly defined role, a.k.a. some sort of work. Work gives us identity, meaning, and defines our lives.

People have a fundamental desire for work.

Gallup, a leading polling organization, has confirmed this in a survey of thousands of people across the world. In his book, *The Coming Jobs War*, Jim Clifton (the CEO of Gallup) says, "The primary will of the world is no longer about peace or freedom or even democracy; it is not about having a family, and it is neither about God nor about owning a home or land. The will of the world is first and foremost to have a good job. Everything else comes after that."[2]

We seek the most important aspects of life (such as money, meaning, and freedom) from the work we do. There is a profound change going on for such an important element of our lives.

Work as we know it is being disrupted today. The revolutionary technologies of the 21st century are not just disrupting industries; they are also disrupting the work of individuals. Technology-led automation is killing most of the traditional jobs and radically redefining the remaining jobs.

If there is one clear trend that the world is moving towards, it is automation. Everything that humans possibly could do for a

11

living is being taken away by automation. Every new technology brings us a step further in this trend, relieving humans from the burden of work and—more and more often—from their making a living, too.

Revolutionary technologies seem to bring new possibilities, promising employment opportunities, and often create new industries, as well. If you examine the overall purpose behind the evolution of technology, it's always toward doing something better or eliminating the need for the current way of doing things altogether. This is not a recent trend, but a phenomenon evident since the dawn of civilization.

A Brief History of Work

In the prehistoric period, apart from a few primitive tools used in their hunting, foragers had practically no external means for doing their work. Foragers lived in a society where there was 100 percent work and zero percent automation. This was the period when every living human was an entrepreneur—earning his/her own living with practically no help from society, at least in their adult life.

There was no transactional relationship that bonds one human to work for another, so any available tools were only used to ease the work of the individual. The relationship between technology and work was confined to individuals.

About 11,500 years ago, sophisticated tools were used to ease *collective* human work when agriculture was developed, the first time this had been done. The phenomenon of foragers adapting to agriculture was a great inflection point in the evolution of technology and for human civilization in general. Agricultural technology helped to eliminate hard labor and create more food. It was the first societal system that created a well-defined meaning for the term "work for a living."

Agrarian society prevailed for almost 11,000 years, with more than 90% of the people working in the fields to produce food. The remaining people were either in the ruling class or people working in other professions. However, the default means of survival was still predominantly entrepreneurship, except for the fact that a cohesive *family* was engaged together in their means of production (unlike each individual striving for food, as it had been in the forager's society).

This was the period when technology-led automation helped people to make their *society* prosperous, without impacting individual work. Recent studies have shown that the technology of medieval agriculture was always sufficient for the needs of the people under normal circumstances. There are no indications that there was excess productivity due to technological sophistication that led to job losses.

The industrial revolution in the 18th century was the next big leap towards automation. At that time, apart from food, other fundamental human needs (such as clothing, transportation, communication, and a whole lot of merchandise) were produced on a scale never heard of before, thanks to that technological revolution.

Over the next three centuries, Western society has increasingly shifted from agricultural work to wage-earning employment in an industrial environment. Technology has created more jobs and opportunities in multiple ongoing and newly-created industries. But during this period, there was also a silent but significant trend: work (the essential thing one does for survival) had increasingly moved outside of family-owned entrepreneurship.

People became wage-earners, and entrepreneurship shrank to less than 10% of the population. People migrated to cities, where they could find work and a seemingly better lifestyle.

Any technology-driven automation in family-based entrepreneurial activities eased their manual labor, which helped them to produce more with less effort and without linking work to the individual's survival.

The Shift to Capitalism Led to the Race for Work

In a family-led entrepreneurship, lack of work due to any sort of automation leads to more freedom and personal enjoyment. In family-owned agrarian societies, since human effort was not measured by an hourly rate, any predisposition for enjoying their time at the cost of avoiding work was treated with empathy and love within the family unit. However, the motives of capitalist entrepreneurs were different. Their single objective was profit, so they wanted to increase productivity while reducing labor cost.

Technology-led automation was seen as a savior for capitalists because—*with* automation—they could produce more output with less human work, thereby decreasing labor cost.

In the early years of the industrial revolution, jobs were increasing because the industry was just forming up and there was a lot to produce and sell, but by the early 20th century, industrialized countries started experiencing overproduction and diminishing demand that ultimately led to the Great Depression.

Due to the capital-intensive nature of the industry, people could only survive if they could find work in the companies, because they did not have any other entrepreneurial opportunities. When the companies struggled to sell their goods, they had no option but to lay off employees. During the Great Depression, the race for work had begun on a grand scale.

The only way for companies to survive was to produce and sell more. British economist John Maynard Keynes suggested that increasing demand is the only way to revive an economy. The solution was to sell more, so we invented marketing and advertising.

The Consumer Becomes a Driving Force in the Economy

Before the Great Depression, the word "consumption" had a negative connotation, meaning the act of *consuming*, through use, decay, or destruction. Companies actively promoted their products through advertising, which gradually changed the cultural fabric of society. Increasing consumption began to be perceived as a positive trend, one to be greatly encouraged.

One's personal success and fame was increasingly recognized on the basis of one's personal possessions (material wealth/net assets and tangible goods), a major shift in human belief system that was accomplished through the science of marketing and advertising.

The drive for increased consumption and productivity led to increased automation, which led to less and less work for humans. Today, an average worker needs to work a mere 11 hours per week to produce as much as one that worked 40 hours per week in 1950.

Today this excess of productive time is spent either on producing more (by those who are lucky enough to have jobs) or going jobless (by those who are not employable). In this same period, working for others has become essential for the majority of the population, leaving no escape from either of these two options.

Defining Moments for Work and Technology

The growth of productivity is being increasingly disconnected from the labor force. Between 1950 and 2000, the global *population* has increased from 2.5 billion to 6.1 billion, i.e. 2.4

times[3]. During the same period, the global GDP has increased from about $4 trillion dollars to $41 trillion dollars, i.e. more than 10 times[4]. Where did this tenfold increase come from? It came from increased productivity in those organizations that were equipped with automation.

In order to understand the emerging relationship between human work and technology, I divide the entirety of human history into five major periods, as shown in the table below. In every period, there was a dominant resource used, through which civilization evolved.

There was a clearly-defined *social revolution* that defined the rules for growth and survival. There was at least one *major invention* that became the pivotal point in each of these historical periods. I divided the entire history into these five periods, based on the birth of these inventions, because they eventually changed everything that occurred later.

Another noticeable attribute of these periods is the type of economy that prevailed. People depended heavily on one major entity to grow economically. Combining all of these views, we can clearly see where we are heading to in the next century.

Evolution	First	Second	Third	Fourth	Fifth
Period	70000 BC to 10000 BC	10000 BC to 1700 AD	1700 to 1900	1900 to 2000	2000 ~
Dominant Resource	Nature	Land	Capital	Knowledge workers	Artificial Intelligence
Social Revolution	Communities	Religion	Politics	Finance	Network of people & AI
Big Invention	Language	Nation-state	Bank	Corporation	Technology convergence
Type of Economy	Entrepreneurial	Agricultural	Industrial	Information	Entrepreneurial

70,000 BC to 10,000 BC

According to historical estimates, *Homo sapiens* developed language and started sharing complex ideas with others around 70,000 BC. This was the major turning point in the history of evolution that ultimately led an insignificant animal to become a dominant species on this planet.

Humans lived in small communities, with everyone living almost independently as an entrepreneur when it came to one's own survival. The capabilities of our prehistoric ancestors were limited, so they had to depend largely on the providence of nature for food and shelter. There were hardly any tools, so everyone had to work hard to find food often enough, either independently or in small groups. Life was pretty much the same until agriculture began around 10,000 BC.

10,000 BC to 1700 AD

Agriculture transformed human life and brought social, cultural and technological revolutions. Organized work for survival became part of daily life. Fertile land became the primary source of food, so it became the dominant resource. Land had a strong influence on the overall progress of the human race.

Evolution of complex ideas led to the development of various religions, often to protect the land and harvested food. Settlements around fertile lands led to larger communities (in the form of nation states) that accelerated the growth of population, settlements and even competition for creating and controlling wealth.

1700 AD to 1900 AD

Agricultural societies maintained a more or less similar lifestyle until the industrial revolution started, around 1700 AD. The

17

next 200 years of the industrial era created a new social order and cultural change. Industries thrived on capital, making it the dominant resource of those times.

In order to support the need for larger sums of capital, banks were invented. As power was shifting from land to industry and capital, nations had to forgo their grip on authoritarian rule and accept a democratic administration of society, which in turn led to politics ruling the land, rather than religion or kingdoms.

1900 AD to 2000 AD

The 20th century was actually a transition period into a larger change that is now looming in the 21st century. Although capital was still an important ingredient in the economy, intellectual property drove the growth of industries.

The need for larger capital investment into research and expansion across the globe drove the formation of corporations. Corporations are immortal and they do not depend on any single individual or nation for survival. Thanks to the availability of banks, capital was liberally available.

Given the equal amount of capital being accessible to different companies, intellectual property defined their success in the market. This led from a merely industrial economy to the emergence of the information economy.

2000 AD and afterward

With the dawn of 21st century, the social, political and economic forces that governed the 20th century are losing their strength. *Intellectual property is no longer a dominant resource because information is widely accessible to everyone.*

The time window for proprietary knowledge is shrinking because people are able to replicate innovative things, thanks to the maturation and convergence of multiple disruptive technologies. When it's time for machines to take up most of the cognitive work at near-zero marginal cost and efficiencies are beyond human reach, no amount of capital and information can compete with them in creating economic value.

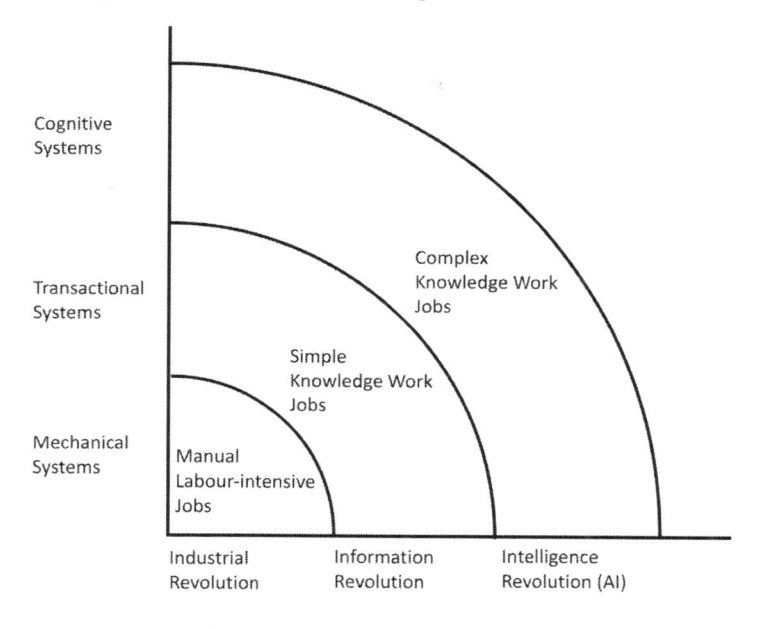

Figure 1. Impact of automation on human work at each stage of major technological revolutions

The dominant resource in 21st century is Artificial Intelligence. It is going to drive both cognitive and physical tasks, using the embedded intelligence in information systems and the rapidly growing use of robots. People, corporations and nations that have access to this privileged superpower can lead the world from the front. As shown in figure 1, earlier technology revolutions have relieved humans from hard manual labour and some of the knowledge work. With the oncoming AI revolution, complex knowledge work is also being taken away by machines.

What differentiates among corporations and nations is their ability to build abundant energy, transportation, manufacturing and computing resources, using technology convergence. The total society is increasingly becoming boundary-less and identity-less because of the growing network of people and machines that spans and interrelates all of the seemingly isolated societies in today's world.

The True Colors of Automation

The growing abundance from the disruptive technologies is creating a threat to capitalism and making corporations irrelevant in the market place. New forms of value and new rules of exchanging that value are emerging, such as bitcoin and social commerce. (I will discuss this more in later chapters.)

When machines were becoming sophisticated and able to do a lot more work than what was previously done by humans, the last thing that humans expected to do was to find themselves *working with* those sophisticated machines.

But what if those machines can communicate with other machines and accomplish tasks without human support? What if machines can think, and their combined intelligence surpasses human intelligence? What if machines can produce things, using available raw materials and designs, without any need for human effort?

This is already happening today on different scales, and the fire of change is moving quickly.

In 1962, when General Motors introduced the first industrial robot (Unimate) for welding auto bodies together, automation had quietly slipped into the manufacturing industry. Today manufacturing is totally different from what it was 50 years ago. Some of the assembly lines are completely managed by robots. I suggest you watch the YouTube video about manufacturing

Tesla cars: https://www.youtube.com/watch?v=8_lfxPI5ObM. Humans are rarely found in modern manufacturing plants.

Don't think that automation only applies to low-skill, mechanical jobs. While robots are chasing blue-collar employees, AI is invading the creative realm. In March 2016, Japan accepted a book written by a machine as a valid submission for their prestigious Hoshi Shinichi Literary Award. We are in the transition period where AI is taking over human intelligence in certain niches. No occupation is safe.

Your present bread-winning skill may not help you make a living 5 years from now. Automation is not limited to mundane jobs. In fact, it replaces skilled jobs and cognitive tasks faster than mundane jobs. The threat is imminent for white collar-workers, too. This is the basis for the Race for Work, in which many will be left behind and fall to the side. You don't have to be one of them!

McKinsey & Co. recently estimated that 45% of today's work activities could be done by robots, AI or some technology.[5] In March 2016, Bryan Dean Wright, a former CIA covert operator, reported in the *LA Times* that United States White House economists had released a forecast that calculated more precisely who is going be put out of work by various forms of automation.[6] Most occupations paying less than $20 an hour will be automated into obsolescence.

The World Economic Forum 2016 report says that disruptive technologies will destroy 7.1 million jobs across the world by 2020, with only 2.1 million of those being replaced by new jobs created from these technologies. When it comes to disrupting skills, the report says that up to 40% of the top skills required for most of today's jobs will change in the next 5 years.[7] Some professors argue that we could see 50% unemployment within 30 years.[8]

21

Exploring the risks of job automation to developing countries, the Oxford Martin School and Citi released a report that claimed estimated job losses ranging from 55% in Uzbekistan to 85% in Ethiopia—a substantial share in major emerging economies, including 77% in China and 69% in India.[9] Sounds scary, doesn't it?

Among these studies, I particularly like the work done by the researchers at Oxford University and Deloitte. Their study, published in 2013, revealed that about 35% of current jobs in the UK will be at high risk due to automation over the next 20 years[10]. Based on this data, BBC has created an interactive page where you can check the level of risk your job carries due to upcoming automation. Check it out now: http://www.bbc.co.uk/news/technology-34066941

The ultimate result of this phenomenon is going to be a major change in the economy, shifting it towards individual entrepreneurship, which would mean that every individual could tap publicly available resources and create value in society.

Automation Like Never Before

Historically, increased automation has led to creation of more jobs than those that became extinct. However, for the first time in human history, this trend seems to be reversed. The automation we see today is eating away more jobs than it creates. In a research study, economist Jared Bernstein showed that productivity and employment were decoupled at the turn of the millennium.[11]

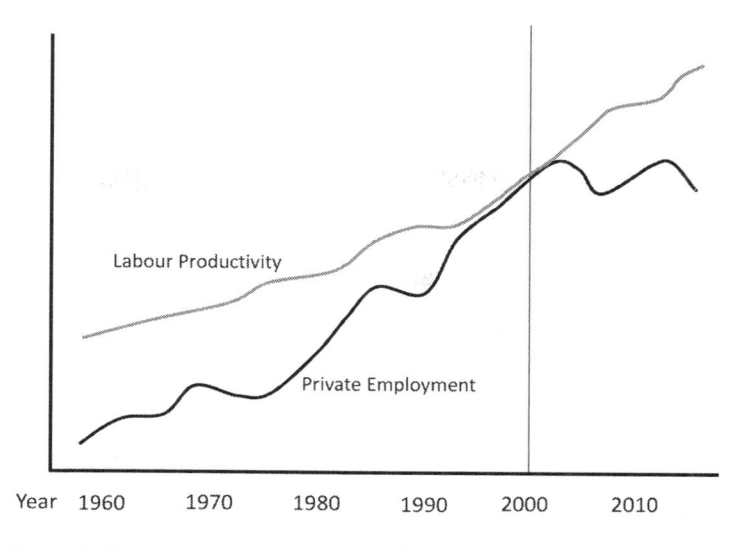

Figure 2. Productivity growth decouples with employment growth in around 2000

Due to increased automation, productivity continued to move upwards but employment was unable to catch up. In fact, in the new millennium, every new automation that has arrived via disruptive technologies is eliminating millions of jobs without adding any significant number of new jobs.

The effect of job loss due to automation is clearly evident in the manufacturing industry. Manufacturing employment has been falling across the globe, including China. The common belief that US manufacturing jobs are being lost to China is no longer valid. Both the American and Chinese workforce is being shrunk, thanks to automation[12].

Outsourcing Is No Longer Lucrative

Outsourcing is yet another reason that is commonly quoted to explain the job losses in the developed world. It is also losing its credibility, because automation is going to claim its role. The

23

majority of the work that is outsourced is relatively routine and well-structured, which can easily be put into an algorithm and automated.

In fact, when organizations now consider outsourcing, automation is more attractive because they don't want to depend on somebody else when they can do it better and cheaper internally. Now that the technology has matured enough to provide for automation, the business case for outsourcing is becoming progressively weak. So, in the unstoppable journey towards automation, outsourcing is just a way station, which eventually has to be phased out.

Leading outsourcing companies in India have realized this fact. Most of them have already started investing heavily in AI, resulting in a massive erosion of low-skilled jobs in India. Infosys is developing its AI platform (called MANA) that can automate repetitive tasks, such as common coding, testing and project management activities.[13] Wipro is working on their AI platform (called Holmes) that is expected to eliminate around 3,000 engineers from mundane software maintenance activities.[14] By adopting automation, another leading IT firm (Tech Mahindra) has set a target of ramping down their headcount by 1200–1400 by March of 2017.[15]

No One Is Spared From Automation

Do you think I'm talking about futuristic technologies and opportunities that are only relevant for software professionals and other tech savvy people? Not at all. The scope of these technologies is far-reaching and the opportunities are for everyone.

In fact, it does not matter whether you are a software professional, involved in technical or non-technical functions in an industry, or working on business support functions, such as finance, HR, procurement, marketing, etc. You are in the midst of golden career opportunities that arise from implementing these disruptive technologies.

Software is eating the world. Many of the traditionally-existing hardware tools and equipment are being replaced by software, either partially or completely. For example, in less than 10 years, iPhone has replaced more than 30 things that we used to carry or use in our homes or offices. Think of an alarm clock, watch, notebook, books, etc. You can find all of them in your smart phone and don't need to carry the physical version of them anymore.

Today the distinction between software and hardware is becoming blurred. 20 years ago, a car was 99% mechanical in nature, with the remaining content comprising electrical and negligible electronics. Today over 40% of the functions in cars are controlled and operated by software. The trend toward self-driven cars will only increase that figure.

This does not mean that all manufacturers are producing the software to augment their hardware products. They are outsourcing from the most cost-effective providers, possibly only until they find out how to automate it. So who is experiencing the effects of that decision? It is the existing employees who carry out various roles in these manufacturing companies.

The case with service organizations is the same. Think of the hospitality industry, tourism, entertainment, etc. Technology is everywhere. Almost all of the professionals are bound to use some sort of software to do their jobs effectively.

Irrespective of the role you play in an organization, you are bound to use some information systems, and you depend on those systems for your productivity as well as the output you create for the organization. These systems are now up for overhaul. You can be the director of the creative operations team that is needed to take on this overhaul job.

Productivity is for robots. To be relevant in this economy, humans need to find a better role for themselves.

I can guess what you were thinking when I said job losses were due to automation. Our immediate history contradicted this prediction. We thought computers were going to eliminate jobs, but they in turn helped economies to thrive by creating more jobs.

According to a 2015 report from Kleiner, Perkins, Caufield & Byers (KPCB), based on data from US Census Bureau, jobs grew 1.7x faster than population from 1948 to 2000, but this trend reversed around 2000. Since 2000, jobs have grown only 0.42x the growth in population[16].

As productivity improved, people started moving from blue-collar jobs to white-collar jobs. In 1862, 90% of the global workforce were farmers. By the 1930s, this number came down to 21%. Today it's less than 2% in the developed world and it's rapidly going down in the developing countries, too.

Technology has been helping us in two different ways. First, it is helping us solve problems. This is usually the result of a focused effort or research aimed at solving certain problems what we already know about.

The second is that, while solving our known problems, it is helping us create possibilities. The fastest ways to travel, the quickest ways to communicate with each other, the ability to manufacture millions of products in a few hours—all of these are new possibilities that our prehistoric ancestors could not have possibly imagined.

When we think of new technology that is going to automate some of the manual work and eliminate jobs, it is these new possibilities that are creating new jobs for us. More possibilities are leading to more applications of such technologies, which in turn creates more jobs.

However, over the same period, technology is getting smarter. Some technologies have become smarter to the extent that they can build on themselves, without human intervention. *When these technologies can outsmart human capabilities and can build on themselves further, humans are no longer needed in the game.*

The technologies that are getting smarter and outperforming humans in both the physical and mental realms are changing the rules of the game, hence reversing the trend of increasing jobs with increasing automation.

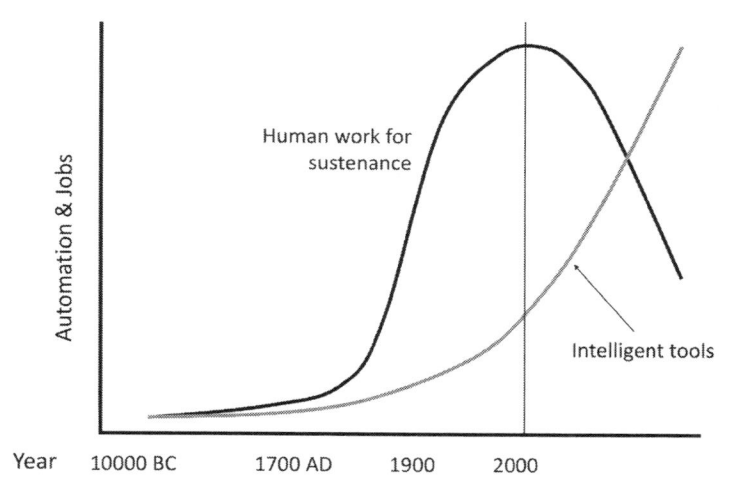

Figure 3: The growth and subsequent fall of the need for a human to work for his sustenance, over recorded history.

As shown in figure 3, until the year 2000, the intelligent tools that humans had made have created more jobs than they replaced, but the trend is shifting now because of the nature of the technology we have today. Intelligent tools are now displacing more jobs than they create.

The Technological Singularity

We are at a technological inflection point that has never occurred before. The change is so rapid that we are quickly moving towards a technological singularity—a situation when machines outsmart humans. American author, inventor and futurist Raymond Kurzweil predicts that it can occur by 2045.

This singularity arises from a period of unprecedented change. It's a change that makes all the existing rules irrelevant. That's why it is not possible to predict the events on the other side of singularity. The "Big Bang" is considered a moment of singularity because all of the laws of physics become invalid before the singularity, and hence we do not know and cannot predict what happened before the Big Bang.

Scientists have identified the events that occurred within a fraction of a second after the Big Bang. And then we could trace our history all the way from that fraction of a second to 13.7 billion years later, which is the age of the universe. Similarly, it is also possible to know what's going to happen *before* the technological singularity, although we cannot predict exactly what will happen after that.

Although the technological singularity is a culminating effect of multiple exponential technologies, the foundation to this future world is being built by three fundamental technologies: AI, IoT and 3D printing. The combined effect of these three technologies can surpass the intellectual and physical abilities of humans. Other disruptive technologies such as Virtual Reality, Robotics, and Synthetic Biology etc. are emerging predominantly because of these three fundamental technologies. That is why I call them "The Big 3 Technologies."

While the world is busily on its way to that singularity, the immediate impact on individuals is the job losses that arise because of increased automation from these technologies. Job losses due to automation have become a topic of interest for research institutes and governments across the globe.

The Big 3 Technologies

With this unprecedented automation, our capitalist society is slowly becoming an unsustainable system. The race for work has steadily increased over the last 100 years and it is about to reach unsustainable levels very soon, primarily because of three disruptive technologies that are already creating havoc in some industries. As mentioned above, I call them "The Big 3 Technologies." They are: the Internet of Things (IoT), Artificial Intelligence (AI) and 3D Printing. The combined effect of The Big 3 Technologies is going to transform the world beyond our ability to imagine.

With IoT technology, not only computers and machines, but practically any "thing" under the sun can be connected to the Internet. The immediate result of this connectivity is the capability to *monitor* what's going on with machines and things. That looks like fun and doesn't pose any threat to us, does it?

But there is a silent intelligence that is slowly growing with this phenomenon. Everything connected to the Internet is producing data on an unimaginable scale. All of the connected things can potentially interact with each other and become intelligent, using the cheaply available AI in the cloud.

With continuously improving capabilities in Big Data processing, we already see magical improvements in AI. Raymond Kurzweil predicts that AI will match the human mind by 2025 and surpass the intelligence of the entirety of humanity by 2029. Kurzweil is not just a futurist who writes science-fiction stories. By the end of the year 2009, 89 of his 108 predictions had proved entirely correct, and all but one of the remaining predictions are already technically feasible; they could happen at any time.

Once AI is built and deployed in the computing cloud, it's available to everyone for free. It's difficult to estimate precisely all that AI can do and who will lose jobs, but we can see that it will impact the very nature of work and the types of industries that exist.

3D Printing is another equally powerful technology that allows the manufacturing of physical objects directly from a software program and basic raw materials. Because of its specific methods, it is also called Additive Manufacturing. 3D Printing is the process of printing physical objects, layer by layer, based on a digital file. It needs as little as 10% of the raw materials that are expended in traditional manufacturing, with tremendous savings in costs. There is no need for extensive planning, preparation of machines, and lengthy manufacturing processes. And the best part is that you can print anything, using practically any material: plastic objects, multi-metallic components, food, human body parts, cars, and buildings. Here, your imagination is the only limit.

These are just a few of the many disruptive technologies that are looming in the scientific laboratories and corporate research centers today. Robotics, Synthetic Biology, and Virtual Reality are among other technologies that are going to have an equally powerful impact on our lives.

Big 3 Technologies in Action

It makes clear sense how automation can take away our jobs in certain industries, such as manufacturing, outsourcing, etc., but many people think it will have no impact on their industry or specifically on their job. As I mentioned before, no one avoids automation, so no industry is immune to this trend. Let me take some counter-intuitive industries and explore how automation, primarily driven by The Big 3 Technologies, is taking away jobs there.

Health care

The health care industry is heavily dependent on human experience and expertise. We all want to go to the most experienced doctor when we are ill. This very dependency on extensive knowledge is opening the door to super-intelligence that will take over our doctors' jobs. The industry analyst firm IDC estimates that 30 percent of health care providers use cognitive analytics by 2018[17].

AI is particularly good at diagnosis. Kurzweil says that deep learning algorithms are just as effective as humans at detecting cancer from ultrasound images and in identifying cancer in pathology reports.

In a 2016 study, Regenstrief Institute found that open-source machine learning tools were as good as or better than humans at "extracting crucial meaning from free-text (unstructured) pathology reports and detecting cancer cases."[18] Samsung recently introduced Medison's RS80A ultrasound imaging system, which features a built-in deep-learning algorithm for breast lesion analysis, almost eliminating the need for a human doctor.

Medical equipment is getting connected to the Internet using IoT capabilities and tapping the power of AI on the cloud, while 3D printing finds its applications in printing human body parts.[19] The health care of tomorrow will be unimaginably different from what we saw even a few decades ago.

Insurance

The job of an insurance agent is all about suggesting a suitable insurance product and then trying to sell it. If you can access the necessary data about your potential customer, the process of identifying the most suitable policy can be reduced to an algorithm.

Insurify, an MIT spinout start-up company, has done this effectively. As an Insurify user, you first text a photo of your license plate to EVIA (Expert Virtual Insurance Agent). EVIA sends you a text with personalized policy quotes and even gives you recommendations, based on your driving history and personal information.

Both the behaviors of humans and the circumstances they get into are being datafied, using IoT technology to estimate risk at an individual level and compute insurance premiums. No human can possibly do this job when complete data and sufficient computing power is available.

Law

Technology has not left behind even the most diehard legal assistants. In fact, they usually have to go through thousands of legal records to prepare for their cases. AI effectively comes to their help.

In May 2016, global law firm Baker & Hostetler announced a new hire: Ross, the world's first artificially-intelligent lawyer. Futurism describes Ross, the brainchild of IBM Watson, as having been designed to "read and understand language, postulate hypotheses when asked questions, research, and then generate responses (along with references and citations) to back up its conclusions." Ross also learns from experience, gaining speed and knowledge the more you interact with it."[20]

The more complex and challenging a task is for the human mind, the easier it is for AI. IoT feeds AI with the data necessary to build intelligence. 3D printing rapidly speeds up this entire process of creating products. Starting with the tasks that are beyond human capacity, the Big 3 Technologies have started nibbling away at the simple and easy tasks, as well.

It's Time to Embrace Work 2.0

For remuneration, rewards and recognition, humans have been historically measured on their productivity at their workplace, but today we are competing with intelligent machines, and there is no way we can beat machines on productivity.

It's time for us to leave productivity to the machines and look for Work 2.0, something that only humans are privileged to do.

What could that be? What can save us from intelligent machines?

Despite the widespread job losses due to automation, there are still pockets of opportunities for us. There are still jobs left for us—well, at least until we all run into that technological singularity. I wanted to write this book to explore those opportunities and reliable ways to achieve them. It is based on my own experience, people I have interviewed, and dozens of books I have read on this topic.

As in any previous situation, there are some skills that are in demand and some other skills that are becoming irrelevant at any point of time in human history. Within that perspective, this period is no different. It's important for everyone to understand which skills are in demand today and how they are going to fare in our generation.

It's time to look into the future of work (Work 2.0), identify the skills that define us as humans, and preserve our place in this world.

Answer the following questions to stimulate your thinking about your own situation:

1. What's the dominant resource in the 21st century? How do you leverage it for your career growth?
2. Is your job at the risk of automation? How do you know?

3. Are you still measuring your success at workplace in terms of productivity? How do you offload that to intelligent machines and look for other ways to differentiate your contribution to your organization?

4. Will your organization survive these changes, or will you have to become part of another one?

Chapter 2. Abundance at the Cost of Jobs

> *"The machine does not isolate man from the great problems of nature but plunges him more deeply into them."* — Antoine de Saint-Exupéry

We are in the age of abundance. Some of the valuable things that you were purchasing a decade ago are available for free today. Disruptive technologies are bringing this abundance. New capabilities, such as long-distance communication and tools to create, replicate and publish content, were beyond our imagination as little as fifty years ago. We have seen all of these capabilities slowly becoming ubiquitous, and by the end of 20th century, many were available for free.

In his book, *Abundance*, author Peter Diamandis explains (with supporting data) how we are entering into an abundant world. He defines abundance as "a world of nine billion people with clean water, nutritious food, affordable housing, personalized education, top-tier medical care, and non-polluting, ubiquitous energy."[21]

While that looks like a utopia, he also estimates a timeline for the world to reach this utopian state, saying that it should be achievable within 25 years, with noticeable change possible within the next decade. Diamandis highlights the latest technological developments in access to clean water, food production, education, health care, energy and many more, and explains how abundance is being created for everyone.

As recently as just 35 years ago, about 50% of the world's population was living under extreme poverty. By 2015, it had fallen below 15%. It is expected that the number of people in absolute poverty across the world will hit zero by 2030[22].

Max Roser, creator of "'Our World in Data," says: "Even in 1981, more than 50% of the world population lived in absolute poverty—this is now down to about 14%. This is still a large number of people, but the change is happening incredibly fast. For our present world, the data tells us that poverty is now falling more quickly than ever before in world history."[23]

Again, as Diamandis says, despite the fact that hundreds of millions still live in abject poverty, disease and want, this generation of human beings has access to more calories, watts, lumen-hours, square-feet, gigabytes, megahertz and, of course, dollars than any that went before. It is definite that we are heading towards an abundance brought to us by technology.

The Dark Side of Abundance

I wanted to explore the technological revolution supporting this abundance further and see what challenges (yes, I see challenges with abundance, too) and opportunities it brings for individuals from a career point of view. The future is filled with abundance at the societal level, but individuals are going to face hardships because that very abundance is leading to job losses.

We all know that the best things in life are free, but I think the saying was speaking about things offered by "Mother Nature". Today we see that some of the man-made things that are equally beautiful and apparently essential for life are also increasingly available for free. Let's call this phenomenon, "demonetization of the cost of living"—basic needs becoming significantly cheaper or potentially free. It means removing money from the equation.

Abundance brought by disruptive technologies has been bringing down the cost of food, health care, education, entertainment, clothing, transportation, housing, etc. to (believe it or not) **zero**. Clearly, technology is the driving force behind this abundance.

Let's look at all the things we stopped buying in the last 20 years: news from around the globe, music, video, an encyclopedia, weather forecasts, satellite images of any place on earth, TV guides, road maps with driving directions, stock quotes, pictures of just about anything, and the list goes on and on.

In *Abundance*, Diamandis compiled a list of things that we were paying for between 1969 and 1989 and that were available for free today. He calculated the value of these products and services to be worth more than $900,000. The list includes products such as video conferencing, GPS, a digital voice recorder, a 5-megapixel camera, a music player, an encyclopedia, a medical library, etc. Today all of these things are either free or an alternative option is available for free.

So what's wrong if something is available for free? After all that's good for everyone, isn't it?

Absolutely. It's a good thing to have something available for free.

But have you ever thought of what happened to the companies that were previously selling these products? What about the people working in those companies? Do you think those companies are still profitable if they are in the same business today?

Of course not. The math is simple here. If we stop paying for something, the companies dealing with those things go out of business. So if the people working in those companies are not wise enough to choose other paying jobs in time, they eventually become jobless.

Abundance has a dark side, too. When technology brings abundance, it destabilizes and uproots the existing economic system. Economic activity thrives on scarcity.

Given that we are at the cusp of a technological revolution, any combination of disruptive technologies can turn the valuable product your organization sells into an abundantly available one, overnight.

Because of the diversified news channels released by multiple online forums, hundreds of print media companies went out of business in the last two decades. In the USA alone, as a 2015 report from the Brookings Institution shows, the number of newspapers per million population fell from 1800 to 400 in 2015 and circulation per capita declined from 35 percent in the mid-1940s to under 15 percent[24].

In order to make more money, corporations invest capital and create goods and services for which there is a demand. When these goods and services become either freely available or at ridiculously low prices, the capital investment does not make sense, so there is no need for the continued existence of a corporate business to fulfill that need. The entire population that is surviving in that industry will be eventually forced to find other jobs.

Abundance has its price, if you're not prepared for it.

Abundance on an Exponential Growth Path

Okay, whatever has happened so far has no effect on my job, do I still need to worry about this abundance? The answer is a resounding YES.

We are entering into the age of abundance, where many valuable things are going to be abundantly available for near-zero prices. The Big 3 Technologies have the power to absolutely transform some of the precious things that are part of our vital economic system.

Some of the most valuable resources in modern society today are energy, transportation and manufactured goods. In fact, the entire industrial world and modern society have been built on these things over the last 200 years. But this is going to change, thanks to the revolution in harvesting solar energy, backdropped by The Big 3 Technologies.

An abundant energy paradigm fundamentally changes the way we live on this planet. Energy is already on the path of abundance.

The solar power in the Sahara Desert is enough to supply forty times the entire world's current demand for electricity. The cost of solar energy has already dropped to ~$0.03 per kWh. The technology to harvest solar energy and store it in batteries efficiently is closely following Moore's law (which says that the price of computing power drops by roughly 50% every 18 months) and is about to enter the disruption stage, thanks to the discovery of the Perovskite solar cell[25]. Perovskite is a light-sensitive crystal that has the potential to be more efficient, inexpensive, and versatile than all other existing solar solutions to date.

Between 2009 and 2016, perovskite's conversion efficiency has increased exponentially from 4 percent to nearly 20 percent, making it the fastest developing technology in the history of photovoltaics.

This is just the beginning, and the future is even more promising. The theoretical limit of perovskite's conversion efficiency is about 66 percent. Compare that to the efficiency we get from traditional internal-combustion engines (around 20 percent), and you begin to grasp the idea of energy abundance.

3D printing is yet another technology that is accelerating the abundance. It is entering into the disruption stage, where anyone can buy a 3D printer for under $1000 and make most of their household products according to their personal taste. The manufacturing industry is going to face this harsh reality very soon.

We are not going to get energy, transportation and manufactured products totally free anytime soon, but they are no longer going to be scarce resources. The price we will have to pay for them will make commercial businesses irrelevant in the marketplace. Is this not enough to shatter the great corporate empires that are surviving in these industries today? Think of the fate of employees working in those companies.

Abundance Brings Abundant Resources to Create

It is not just about a scarce resource turning into an abundant one. Along with abundance, we need to pay attention to another emerging trend: so-called "Industrial Production" is moving towards "Individual Production."

Let's look at the same example from solar energy. With the ability to harvest solar energy and use it for your daily needs, you don't need to continuously buy it from energy-selling companies. You just need to buy energy-harvesting equipment, such as solar panels and storage batteries. It is a one-time investment, with negligible running costs. Once purchased, you become energy independent. Then you use that energy to drive your battery-powered car, becoming fuel independent. The other modes of transportation also should become far less expensive because of abundant solar energy.

Similarly, 3D printing has the potential to replace trillions of dollars' worth of manufacturing industry activity with individual production—well, at least for some of the goods.

You just need to buy the basic raw materials, which can't be easily overpriced because they are just commodities. The price of commodities is primarily governed by demand and supply dynamics. They are not vulnerable to additional value being added by individuals or organizations.

Individual production is slowly taking away the need for commercial business.

This shift is already being observed in some other areas of our society. How many times have you gone to a photographer in the past year? You can take as many photos as you want from your smartphone and the quality is good enough for most of your daily needs.

Abundance and the shift to individual production are the gifts of the 21st century. However, the very same gifts are leading to shrinking capitalism. Corporations and employees that are affected by these effects have no place to go but to look for other means of providing a living.

Mastering the Two Faces of Abundance

Enough of disappointment. Let's look for some bright side of abundance. We saw that growing abundance can also impact your career and life. Based on some early indications and past experience, you can foresee into the future to some extent. That foresight gives you an opportunity to not only avoid the threats, but to grab the opportunities as well.

How can I be prepared for it? If something is available for free, I will use it anyway. Do I need to plan and get ready for it? Of course, there is no need to be prepared for the free stuff, but that is just one side of abundance. The other side poses threats to your career. You need to learn how to master it.

The good news is that the transition to abundance offers some of the rarest career opportunities for individuals, even though the role of capitalism is shrinking in general. I discuss some of these opportunities in Section 2.

You need to be aware of what's happening in the world with regard to your company and especially with regard to your job. If you sense that abundance is embracing what you produce at your workplace, it's time for you to move on to greener pastures.

Are you already being impacted by abundance? What your company sells is available abundantly out there for free? Then you are already in danger. All I can suggest is to read this book further and act on it immediately.

Answer the following questions to stimulate your thinking about your own situation:

1. The world is getting better. Are you still buying anything that is available for free elsewhere?
2. What's the dark side of abundance? Do you see that effecting your career?
3. Is your company or (specifically) your job affected by abundance? How do you master abundance?

Chapter 3. Capitalism Got Disrupted

> "Capitalism forgets that life is social. And the kingdom of brotherhood is found neither in the thesis of communism nor the antithesis of capitalism, but in a higher synthesis."
> — Martin Luther King, Jr.

Although capitalism existed for many centuries as a simple form of trade between people and nations, the meaning we attribute to it emerged from agrarian capitalism in 16th-century England. Colonization shaped the agrarian capitalism into mercantilism. Later, industrialization transformed the mercantilism into industrial capitalism. It lasted until the middle of the 20th century, when the modern globalized capitalism emerged.

We have seen some of the technologies that emerged in the 20th century disrupting various industries. However, the new millennium has positioned capitalism itself to be the next system to be disrupted. The ground for capitalism is shaking because the fundamental rules on which it was built are changing. Embracing disruptive technologies is the way to survive in this economy of collapsing capitalism.

Capitalism Meets Creative Destruction

500 years of capitalism as we know it is being transformed today. Capitalism is being disrupted. Capitalism was built on two pillars: capital and scarcity. Both of these pillars are losing their original meaning today. Capital (a.k.a. money) is being disrupted. Scarcity is being replaced with abundance, thanks to disruptive technologies.

The 20th century has seen the emergence of capitalistic societies across the world. Towards the end of 20th century, Eastern countries such as China and India adopted an unfettered market economy and started realizing massive growth. Today, thanks to capitalism, we have over 2 billion people in the middle class and a few million people in the super-rich class[26].

A few remaining countries are still following non-capitalistic ideals, but they are not so different from the truly capitalistic countries. Today we think that capitalism is by far the best model for economic prosperity and development of the nations, but that is about to change.

Wage-earning has become the default way of living for the middle class, except for a minority of small business owners. According to Joseph Schumpeter, one of the most influential economists of the 20th century, capitalism is the most successful economic system invented by humans so far, because it benefits the entire population by raising their living standards. Ironically, Joseph also popularized "creative destruction," a concept to denote an endogenous replacement of the old ways of doing things through using creative approaches by innovative entrepreneurs and thereby destroying the capitalist structure itself.[27] We see this creative destruction in action in today's economy.

Capitalism as we know it is not going to survive, for many reasons. Creative destruction leads to corporations achieving smaller and smaller profit margins, ultimately forcing them to shut down their business altogether.

Who is going to be impacted most if such a thing happens?

I am sure entrepreneurs with millions of dollars invested in a business would have saved enough for their survival in the event of a bankruptcy. Those who cannot escape would be the working class; they do not have any fall-back option.

There are some strong indications that pose a threat to capitalism as we know it today, and these are only going to increase, thanks to the exponentially-growing and disruptive technologies.

The Great Grip: 5 Ways Consumers Avoid Markets and Become Self-sustaining

Capitalism survives on demand for buying, but buying is never a first choice for consumers, because they need to forgo money first for anticipated value later. Nothing can have more concrete value than the money one holds at any given time.

It is either the perceived higher value than that of the money itself or dire need that encourages consumers to buy things from the market. When consumers have alternate options where they don't need to forgo money, they have no motivation to buy things from the markets. Technology is bringing these new options today, enabling consumers to avoid markets, which leaves capitalism at risk.

There are five ways consumers can get a better deal than buying things from commercial organizations. I call it the "The Great Grip," because these five ways act like a choking hand. They can choke capitalism to death, if it cannot reinvent itself. They are:

1. Let's share what we have.
2. Let technology do it for us.
3. Let's make it together.
4. I can do it myself.
5. Let's buy the best, but only when we need it most.

1. Let's share what we have.

Sharing is as old as human history, but its sheer scale was never bigger than today. Practically every economically valuable resource is being made available for sharing, thanks to the enabling technologies.

The Sharing Economy

An average car is unused 92% of the time because an individual owner does not need to drive it all the time. At the same time, there are millions of people who either do not own a car or do not have access to their own car when they need it.

What if you can just use any car available on the road whenever you need it? Welcome to the sharing economy.

In March 2009, Travis Kalanick and Garrett Camp saw an opportunity to make finding a taxi better and easier than what the taxi industry was offering. They went ahead and founded Uber, a mobile taxi-hailing company, in Silicon Valley. In less than 3 years, it had secured $44.5 million in funding and started expanding outside of the USA. In less than 6 years, it spread to 58 countries and was estimated to be worth over $60 billion. In October of 2014, Uber gave three times more car rides in San Francisco than all cab rides combined.

This phenomenal growth has inspired thousands of start-ups worldwide to copy their business model and apply it not only to the taxi industry, but also to various other industries. In fact, this trend is often called "Uberification," which established a new economy, called "The Sharing Economy."

The sharing economy has rapidly spread to individuals sharing valuable goods like homes, other automobiles, expensive clothes, jewelry, and even food.

AirBnB is disrupting the hotel industry. People with extra rooms in their homes can post their availability on the AirBnB website for people looking for lodging in that particular place and style. AirBnB has more rooms available in New York than all the hotels combined.

Forbes estimated that the revenue flowing through the sharing economy would surpass $3.5 billion in 2013, with growth exceeding 25%.[28]

The sharing economy does not survive just because of cost advantages. When people share their possessions, you not only get them cheaper; you also have access to a lot more variety, which corporations simply can't provide.

There is no reason to believe that the sharing economy is just a fad. This is going to be there in this form (at least in our generation) until we find better ways to share our valuable possessions.

None of the traditional valuable goods (such as cars, homes and clothes) are exempted from the sharing economy. So where can a corporation escape to and be able to survive? It is obviously into something that the sharing economy can't do or provide. My answer is, "the disruptive technologies." Corporations are good at bringing innovative goods and services to market that can't be easily copied by individuals, so the growth areas for both corporations and individuals is through embracing the disruptive technologies.

Collaborative Commons

There are multiple online tools available for free to edit text, images, videos, designs, maps, and many other digital goods. When the cost of replicating and modifying things becomes next to zero, anyone can produce and share them with others. We saw this phenomenon in the newspaper industry and publishing industry.

Today billions of people are sharing text, audio and video at near zero cost. In his bestselling book, *The Zero Marginal Cost Society*, author Jeremy Rifkin calls these groups the "collaborative commons." [29]

Internet technologies have made it possible to share information at near-zero marginal cost. Because of this, collaborative commons can produce information and related goods and services at near-zero marginal cost and share them with others practically for free.

While collaborative commons are busy producing stuff without depending on commercial offerings in the market, corporations find fewer and fewer opportunities to sell their goods and services, so they need to become leaner and produce stuff with even greater productivity to maintain their profit margins. They adopt automation wherever possible to eliminate people, ensure quality and consistency, while reducing costs at the same time.

In this scenario, the only place one can find a job, if not a dream job, is to help corporations achieve this mission. Exponential technologies are well placed to serve corporations in this mission and you should embrace them to find your job.

Creative Commons

In 2001, Lawrence Lessig, Hal Abelson, and Eric Eldred founded Creative Commons, a non-profit organization for expanding the range of creative works available for others to legally build upon and to share.

As of November 2014, Creative Commons had enabled authors, artists and designers to create an estimated 880 million works licensed under the various Creative Commons licenses, by sharing and reuse of creativity and knowledge through the provision of free legal and technical tools.

As of March 2015, Flickr alone hosted more than 306 million Creative Commons-licensed photos. If you are a professional photographer, you have dozens of options to sell your photos online to anyone on the planet by uploading your photos to platforms like Flickr, Shutterstock, Dreamstime, etc. This gave birth to an online stock photo industry that is uprooting the traditional photo business.[30]

Access over Ownership

The millennials are different from GenX and baby boomers in many ways. I discuss this more in Chapter 5, but one thing I particularly want to mention here is the millennials' preference to not *own* expensive things such as a house, car, etc., but to *rent* them as needed. They are happy if they can access these things when they need them, but do not particularly dream about owning them in order to show off. This change of behavior is leading to them sharing things instead of owning them.

A survey among US adults conducted by PwC in December 2014 revealed that over 80% of the respondents agreed that sharing valuable things makes life convenient, efficient, affordable and less expensive than owning them.[31]

It is clearly evident that, for millennials, *access* is the new ownership.

This trend is going to dilute the demand for corporate goods and services. The hotel industry is already started to feel the heat from house-sharing habits in society. The taxi industry is facing tough challenges from carpooling and Uber car drivers.

The sharing economy is just beginning. Its impact on the corporate world is yet to be seen in many other industries like manufacturing, textiles, luxury goods, hi-tech, etc. When sharing becomes a preferred choice over ownership, corporations find rapid dilution of demand for their goods and services.

ZipCar, a car-sharing company, recognized the capabilities of IoT technology and the impact of changing social trends from the sharing economy (access over ownership), and came up with an attractive car-sharing model.

ZipCar made all their cars perfectly traceable by embedding sensors and network connections so that they can let anyone pick up their cars from anywhere, without any documentation. If you are a ZipCar member and you need a car—even for an hour—all you have to do is book it online and walk into your nearby ZipCar parking lot. You just need to place your Zip Card against the card reader in the windshield. Voila, the doors open for you and the car is yours. Compare this with the process you need to go through with the traditional rental car companies. You can also understand why people prefer sharing over buying.

2. Let technology do it for us.

Technology is bringing us abundance in computing, communication, and (very soon) transportation and energy. When technology can do it for us for free, we don't need to buy.

Near-Zero Marginal Cost

In market capitalism, organizations invest capital and other resources to create products and services that they can sell for a premium in the market. Organizations continuously focus on improving productivity to reduce costs and thereby increase profits.

In a perfect market economy, the cost of goods gets closer to the marginal cost of production because multiple players compete to sell their products for as little markup over the marginal cost of production as possible. However, the marginal cost of production is continuously decreasing because of the continuous improvements in productivity over hundreds of years.

Disruptive technologies such as the steam engine, electricity, and telecommunications have caused significant improvements in productivity that brought down the marginal cost of production of goods over the last 200 years.

With all these technological advancements, it is possible to reduce the processing costs to near zero if we can avoid the raw material costs. For some of the products such as the typewriter, music player, radio, etc., we have already crossed that barrier with digitalization, where we could eliminate the need to have the physical products thanks to their existence in a digital version.

Once a product is built on digital platform (for example, a book, newspaper or communication platform), replicating it costs practically zero, so we have achieved near-zero marginal cost of production for all digital goods. They can be replicated and sent to anyone on the planet for no additional cost. Now that the software is eating the world, more and more goods are being brought within the scope of digitalization, leaving traditional industries behind and out of business.

As the software is eating the world, we need fewer and fewer physical objects in our daily life. Once something is digitized, it can be produced and shared at zero marginal cost, after which there exists little opportunity for building a profitable business on a capitalist agenda.

Thanks to the evolving IoT, Big Data and 3D printing technologies, more and more physical goods can be produced at near-zero marginal cost.

The next wave of productivity after the steam engine and electricity is going to be triggered by IoT. When the IoT infrastructure is in place, every machine, network and device will be used to its peak performance levels and maintained with real-time support. This leads to a further reduction in the marginal cost of producing goods.

51

During the past decade, rapid upward movement in industrial productivity has been clearly evident.

For example, in its Kentucky facility, Toyota has improved its troubleshooting capabilities by using real-time monitoring and error corrections that minimized rework and scrap. Toyota claims that at their Alabama facility, these improvements have resulted in an annual cost saving of $550,000 in 2012.[32]

The improvement in productivity, coupled with other disruptive technologies, can bring down the cost of today's high-value products that are being sold in the market.

Futurist Ramez Naam has analyzed how cheap electric cars can get. He predicts that by 2030, electric vehicles with a 200-mile range will become cheaper than the least expensive car sold in the U.S.A. in 2015. These prices will come down further as the materials and technologies behind renewable energy continue to improve, leading to accelerated adoption of electric vehicles. Think of the disruption that's going to cause the $9 trillion-dollar automobile industry.[33] What about the oil and gas industry, which is closely associated with the automobile industry?

With 3D printing and IoT infrastructure, anybody can print most of the common goods required in daily life, using locally available materials. We don't need expensive manufacturing equipment and long supply chains to transport goods.

What if the scarce resources (such as manufactured goods, transportation, energy and communication) were actually available to everyone for near-zero marginal cost? These four scarce resources comprise at least 50% of the world's GDP, if not more. The 21st century is all set to witness this reality.

We have seen that innovative entrepreneurs use disruptive technologies to create better and cheaper products, challenging industry stalwarts. Using innovation, many business strategists have tried laying out principles for creating great companies. However, as The Big 3 Technologies take root in society, even entrepreneurship whose backdrop is innovation is also going to be short-lived. When individuals can tap all of the resources needed to create the same products that an innovative start-up can offer, how long can a start-up survive in the market?

In fact, this is already happening in certain segments of the industry. Invisalign (a medical device company headquartered in San Jose, CA) has already demonetized custom tooth aligners ("braces") with its 3D printing process.

While Invisalign is busy planning enhancements to their next product, Amos Dudley (a budget-conscious college student) found a way to demonetize Invisalign braces, using equipment in his school's digital fabrication lab. After some orthodontics research, Dudley bought inert retainer plastic on eBay and used a NextEngine laser scanner, Stratasys Dimension 1200es 3D printer, and a vacuum forming machine to create a set of personalized, homemade aligners. All he spent was $60 on materials. After 16 weeks of wearing them, Dudley's teeth are perfectly straight.

Disruptive technologies are fueling a revolution in solar-energy harvesting, leading to near-zero marginal cost for our energy and transportation needs. Even with technologies available in 2016, if you can invest in a properly sized solar electric system, your home or office can be a net-zero power plant, producing enough clean energy on a yearly basis to meet all of your electricity needs and break even on your investment in less than 4 years.[34]

Thanks to artificial intelligence from Big Data, coupled with IoT and 3D printing, most of the existing manufacturing industry is going to be irrelevant in the 21st century.

Capitalism was built in such a way that its own success is leading to its fall. The very need for productivity is eroding the reason for the existence of capitalism. When the marginal cost of production approaches near zero due to automation, employees stand to be the first who are removed from this game. In this century, wage-earning professionals are the most affected.

3. Let's make it together.

Ubiquitous computing and communication are helping people to gather the necessary skills and resources to create something valuable for the entire society. We call this phenomenon Social Production.

Social Production

Harvard Law School professor Yochai Benkler coined the term "Commons-based Peer Production" to name the growing phenomenon of large groups of people, often unknown to each other, contributing to massive projects. It's a new model of social production, in which large numbers of people work cooperatively towards a common goal.

These projects have less rigid hierarchical structures than those under more traditional business models. Commons-based projects are usually designed without any need for financial compensation to contributors.

The key attribute of this social production is that the inputs and outputs of the process are shared, freely or conditionally, in an institutional form that leaves them equally available for all to use as they choose, at their individual discretion. This is a serious threat to market capitalism because capitalism thrives on creating scarce resources and selling them for profit. In the age of abundance, there is little room for capitalism.

Massive projects like Linux, Wikipedia, and Open Street Map, etc. are examples of social production.

As of January 2016, Wikipedia has over 38 million articles in approximately 250 languages. It has become such a valuable resource for the entirety of humanity that, in 2012, the founders even debated applying for UNESCO world heritage status for the Wikipedia website.[35]

The voluntary effort that went into building Wikipedia is undeniably significant. However, it's not so significant when one considers the vast pool of free human hours available in this world. For an analogy, it was estimated that in one year, people in the US alone spend a Wikipedia worth of time when watching advertisements every weekend.

If we were to forgo our television addiction for just one year, the world would have over a trillion hours of cognitive surplus. Think of what else we can do and how we can make this world a better place without the help of corporations.

4. I can do it myself.

Do It Yourself (DIY)

Capitalism has taken away the age-old method of "DIY" for most of one's daily needs by creating a commercial product or service. However, the unexpected abundance in many areas of daily life is taking us back to the good old days of DIY. Today, DIY is considered one of the leading risks of organizations because the DIY revolution opens up free tools and services to consumers with which they can fix their problems without any money involved.

Ascent of the Prosumer

During the past 20 years, communication has been democratized by the Internet. However, the recent advancements in IoT, Big

Data and 3D printing are going to democratize energy and transportation—the two key elements of human life—in the next 20 years.

By 2020, the United States is expected to generate 20% of its energy from renewable energy sources. The figures for Europe and China are 20% and 15%, respectively.[36] Most of these sources are owned by small players (and even individuals) who generate energy and supply it back to the grid.

IoT is currently being used in the integration of a distributed energy grid. This leads to massive productivity gains in terms of energy saving because each appliance will be used only when it is required and, if possible, during the off-peak period. For example, washing machines can be programmed to switch on during the off-peak period when there is plenty of excess energy. Smart appliances in the homes and offices can be programmed to switch on only when they are needed, so that they can save energy.

Prosumers, as they are called, are the people who consume and well as generate energy and supply it back to the grid when they do not need it. There has been a steady rise in the number of prosumers in the last five years. Energy is no longer exclusive to the large utility companies. Individuals, small companies, and even large industries can become prosumers.

Regulations are slowly being updated to manage this distributed-energy-generation process. Through legislation, the State of Minnesota (USA) allowed utilities to implement a value of solar (VOS) tariff that gives customers with solar installations credit for the electricity generated by them.[37] With this approach, utility companies can better understand customer load, timing, and volume, because a VOS tariff separates electricity generated by the consumer from electricity consumed.

Utility companies have already become afraid of losing their business to prosumers. They have pro-actively started taking part in this journey before consumers become aware of it.

For example, the Arizona Public Service Electric Company (APS) and Tucson Electric Power (TEP) have successfully negotiated with the Arizona state government to allow them to directly lease their customers' rooftops for solar power generation. In exchange for "renting" their roofs, homeowners will get a credit on their monthly bills for 25 years. APS has offered a $30 monthly credit to a solar customer's bills.[38]

Once the energy internet is in place, prosumers can sell their energy in the competitive markets, challenging traditional big players in the market. More than two hundred years' worth of utility industry dominance is under serious threat today, thanks to the rise of the distributed-energy internet.

A similar trend is visible in the manufacturing industry, although at the moment, it is in its nascent stage. Using 3D printing and IoT technology, anyone can use the publicly-available designs and locally-available cheap materials to print the goods they want and even to sell them in the market.

Thingiverse is one of the popular 3D model repositories where anyone can find pre-made designs of simple products for free. You can further customize these designs, if you want to. Even if you don't own a 3D printer, you can get an object printed by someone who owns one for a nominal price.

In 2009, Chris Anderson, former editor-in-chief of the magazine, *Wired*, started experimenting with 3D printing to produce unmanned aerial vehicles (UAVs). Anderson left *Wired* to start his own company (3D Robotics) in 2012 and made it into a multimillion-dollar enterprise within a few years, disrupting larger organizations in the UAV space.

Anderson used his home-based start-up to introduce these UAVs to the market by embracing 3D printing. Clearly, Anderson is not alone. As other individuals and entrepreneurs begin to adopt 3D printing, the manufacturing industry will be subjected to potentially serious disruption. This is going to challenge the more than $11 trillion manufacturing industry in the next two decades.[39]

5. Let's buy the best, but only when we need it the most.

Technology has definitely not yet developed to the point where it can give us abundant food and resources. We still need to buy a lot of stuff from the market. If there is nothing from the above four options that helps us to avoid the markets for meeting our needs, then there is still some hope.

Technology is enabling us to choose the best among the plethora of choices, often from remote corners of the world, putting all the fluffy things out of business.

Social Commerce

It's a common practice today to check online reviews and suggestions from our friends on social networks before buying products or using services such as restaurants or hospitals, etc. This is called Social Commerce. It is the use of a social network in the context of e-commerce transactions.

This is a fundamental change in buying behavior, thanks to the availability of better information about what we want to buy. Before this phenomenon, we used to depend on local shops and whatever information the shopkeeper gave us when we made our buying choices.

The need for more information in order to make better buying decisions is an irreversible trend. Because consumers' buying decisions are depending a lot more on data, corporates are forced to collect more data, understand it, and then try to influence customers in their favor.

Winner Takes It All

With so much data available about the products and the experiences of consumers with those products, every product eventually builds its own online profile, which is easily accessible to all of those who are interested to check it. Gone are the days when we depended on a salesperson's advice to make our buying decisions. Today we depend on online resources to find the best product in every niche category when we want to buy. No one wants to buy inferior products or services.

If you know what the best is and it's accessible and affordable to you, you do not want to choose even the second best, let alone the rest of them in the top ten, so the market is favorable to only the best in every niche, which leaves less and less business opportunity for the rest. The winner in every business segment essentially takes all of the business.

The more information we can access, the smaller the number of businesses that can survive in the new economy. Capitalism has no place in such a world, where information is uniformly available to everyone and buying decisions are already made before the customer even comes up with a need.

Two-sided Markets

The connected world has broken physical and information barriers between buyers and sellers. Today there is less and less need for middlemen in any business.

With the emergence of e-commerce, we saw new market platforms, where you can purchase goods right from the warehouse, eliminating the need for distributors and salespeople. This elimination of the middlemen directly translates to lower prices for consumers, partly because buyers can bypass their lengthy supply chains.

These economic platforms are called two-sided markets. They usually have two or more distinct user groups that provide each other with the benefit of their network. The more people join the platform, the more useful it becomes for every user. This is called the network effect. Social networking sites like Facebook and LinkedIn have grown to encompass the entire world primarily because of the network effect.

Two-sided networks can be found in many industries, sharing the space with traditional product and service offerings. For example, credit cards connect cardholders and merchants, eliminating the need for separate financing. In the United States, health maintenance organizations (HMOs) connect patients and doctors. "Yellow pages" connect advertisers and consumers. Recruitment sites connect job seekers and those who are hiring, eliminating the need for recruiting agencies; search engines connect advertisers and potential users/buyers.

This is a serious threat to all of those businesses that currently survive by being the interface between the buyer and seller. With the proliferation of two-sided markets, they will be eventually uprooted and greatly diminished in their role.

Dilution of Demand

If there is one thing needed for capitalism to survive, it is demand. The whole system is built on the assumption that, if you produce something, somebody somewhere will need your product or service and be willing to buy it from you. Today, we still need all that we needed yesterday and maybe much more.

The game-changing part is our necessity to buy. The age of abundance has opened up other sources for goods and services. These sources are offering goods and services either for free or at negligible prices, which are usually better and more satisfying for our needs of the day.

Traditional capitalistic businesses are struggling to meet this combination of quality and price because it is almost impossible for them to be profitable if they do.

As the cost of 3D printing technology declines, production becomes local and extremely customized to individual needs. It becomes unviable for large global manufacturing companies to produce at one end of the world and deliver at the other end. Moreover, production may occur in response to *actual* demand, which is usually less than the anticipated or forecasted demand.

Capitalism of the 3rd Millennium

Where is the world heading toward with all these trends? It's hard to imagine a world economy without capitalism. Living standards of the entire world have significantly improved, thanks to capitalism, but there is a lot to improve in the majority of the world. The developed world is still a minority in terms of population.

If capitalism has no place, do we have any better option? Yes, we do, and that's where we are heading. We enjoy abundance from two different sources.

One is from the rise of an economy (due to industrial production and commercial activities) that is largely dependent on capitalism.

The second is the exponential technologies. They are able to bring us ubiquitous computing power and energy, with which we can get most other things abundantly. During the second half of the second millennium, we saw a major increase in living standards that primarily came from the rise of capitalism. The more qualitative version of economic prosperity is the abundant food and access to resources that exponential technologies started to bring us around the turn of the present millennium.

The 3rd millennium is going to be dominated by creating this abundance in every sphere of human existence. Everything will be aligned to this transformative journey, including capitalism.

The concept of money has not changed over the millennia. Blockchain technology, one of the exponential technologies, is disrupting money today. With this, we are moving into a diversified definition of "value," without limiting it to a mere currency. The new-found responsibility of capitalism is to identify better ways of creating and distributing value from the exponential technologies, in order to create abundance in the general society.

Thriving in Disrupted Capitalism

The irony is that the very exponential technologies that are responsible for uprooting capitalism are also offering some golden opportunities for individual career success until capitalism hits its doomsday end.

When a bulldozer is uprooting the contours of the surroundings, what's the better place to stand, apart from the bulldozer itself? Better opportunities accumulate where the business activity accumulates.

In the 21st century, the center of attraction for every business lies with adoption of exponential technologies to gain productivity benefits and create new revenue streams, at least in the short term. This very trend is offering an unprecedented opportunity for job seekers.

When I first decided to write this book, I looked for some help online for writing and self-publishing it. I was surprised to discover so many people who are building a multi-million-dollar business out of helping aspiring authors with writing and publishing books.

This is the age of self-publishing. Millions of books were published on Amazon. A study on author revenues found that less than 10% of self-publishing authors are earning about 75% of the reported revenue and half of the writers are earning less than $500 in a year.[40]

However, those *helping* these first-time authors are making money. There are so many so-called experts in the industry who help would-be authors to come up with an idea for writing a book, create the content, and find help with editing, formatting, cover design, publishing and marketing.

During the gold rush, do not run for gold, but sell spades! If you are an expert in any of these areas, you can potentially earn more than an author, because now there are millions of people all across the world who want to write books, and this number had been skyrocketing ever since self-publishing became possible.

Wise people catch the mad market rush early on and make a business out of it. This trend is not limited to the self-publishing industry alone. I personally experienced it in many other areas.

Online business is another example. Three years ago, I paid over $2,000 for an online course that promised to teach me how to start an online business. You can already see the result of that investment. I didn't have any online business before now. I started my website and blog years before purchasing this course and I was not making money from my website. I understood this game after I paid so much and failed to start an online business.

63

When I realized that all of those who are selling such courses are earning more than typical authors, I decided to write this book before looking for any help from others. The single most difficult and important thing if you want to publish a book is to actually write that book. Once you do that, you can figure out the rest.

Understanding the whole process in a nutshell is good, but taking 6-month-long courses for this is nothing but a distraction. It's often good enough if you talk to an experienced person to understand the game. The rest is in your hands. You need to get out and *act* to see the results.

I am not against taking such courses for learning new skills. I have taken multiple courses, spent thousands of dollars on them, and benefited from them most of the time. In fact, investment in personal improvement is one the best investments that you can make. However, when you understand the game enough and the next step is just to take action, no courses will help you until you act on it.

Answer the following questions to stimulate your thinking about your own situation:

1. Which side of capitalism are you in today? Is your business creating abundance with exponential technologies or being attacked by the Great Grip?

2. Which element of the the Great Grip is threatening your business/career?

3. What's your escape plan? Have you identified any exponential technologies that can create abundance for society that you can become part of?

4. How can you use your experience and skills to enter into something that thrives in this economy?

Chapter 4. An Entrepreneur Wants to Change the World

"Never doubt that a small group of thoughtful, committed citizens can change the world; indeed, it's the only thing that ever has." — Margaret Mead

"Only who will risk going too far can possibly find out how far one can go." – T. S. Eliot

"At first, people refuse to believe that a strange new thing can be done, then they begin to hope it can be done, then they see it can be done — then it is done, and all the world wonders why it was not done centuries ago."
— Frances Hodgson Burnett

While capitalism on the whole is shaking due to the multiple challenges discussed in earlier chapters, there has been an unprecedented rise of entrepreneurship in the past decade. This seems ironic but it is not unusual, because society responds to the short-term changes and is usually oblivious of the longer-term implications.

From the beginning of this century, there have been some dramatic changes taking place, precisely due to the Internet revolution. These market shifts rewrote the rules of entrepreneurship that had existed over the past 200 years, and broke most of the barriers for starting a business. In his book, *End of Jobs*, author Taylor Pearson describes the leading trends for this frenzied pace of entrepreneurship[41]:

1. **Democratization of the means of production:** Production is no longer exclusive to the large companies. You no longer need to invest in large production facilities in order to produce any product today. You can use the existing pool of production facilities that are available at far cheaper costs because of their "pay per use" model. You can outsource practically the entire manufacturing part of your product and still make a profit, provided you have an idea for an innovative product or service.

2. **Democratization of distribution channels:** The connected world has removed the boundaries of proprietary distribution channels. Distributors and producers now have greater access to each other, so that new entrants do not need to invest in new distribution channels; they can use the existing channels, again using the "pay per use" model.

3. **Birth of new markets:** The creativity and innovation from budding entrepreneurs is sustained, thanks to the birth of new markets across the world almost every day.

Let's take a closer look into these trends to see how they affect your employability.

1. Democratization of the Means of Production

Michael Porter said that companies thrive on building core competencies in the chain of value creation, such as raw material sourcing, design, methods of production, distribution channels, etc.

In the past 20 years, we have seen companies find it increasingly justifiable to outsource everything but their core competencies. This phenomenon has led to shrinking core competencies, while promoting the distribution of skills across the world.

Suppliers to outsourcing companies are hungry for more business and they are constantly looking for new prospects.

This phenomenon has led to greater focus on standardizing the products, processes, skills, and even the rules of commerce across the world. It is no longer a personal business relationship between supplier and the outsourcing company, because anyone who understands these rules can get the services from the suppliers to produce things.

Starting a company is no longer exclusive to the ultra-rich people who have access to capital and skilled labor. If you see a demand for any particular product in the marketplace, you can start a company and sell the products without actually manufacturing them in your own factory.

Ten years ago, only big companies could afford to get their manufacturing done in China and subsequently ship the products to market. Today you can find the world's best manufacturers on alibaba.com and get your product shipped on demand without the need to invest in a huge inventory.

All you need is an idea and the right network of people who can support you in building your business. Once you figure out the value of selling any product or service, you can get everything—from design to shipping the final product to the customer—done by the best providers in the marketplace, on a global scale.

Ten years ago, if you wanted to start an e-commerce company, you needed to invest tens of thousands of dollars, procure hardware and software, and hire people to build your website, apart from focusing on your core business, to sell your products. Today you can start selling from day one by subscribing to e-commerce platforms like Shopify for as low as $14 USD a month.

What does that mean for large and established companies? If anyone with a better idea can start a business and compete in the market, existing players are constantly under threat.

67

As it's very difficult to match the innovation and entrepreneurial skills of start-ups, established companies often lose business to these start-ups, at least in part. If you are employed by a business that is facing heat from start-ups, what career prospects do you expect from your employer?

2. Democratization of Distribution Channels

Facebook secured over a billion users in less than a decade. Uber expanded into over 50 countries in less than five years. Traditional companies like GE and IBM took multiple *decades* to spread to a handful of countries.

Just like outsourcing opened the gates for manufacturing of goods and services outside organizational boundaries, distribution channels were democratized, too. The connected world has opened multiple ways for entrepreneurs to reach their customers and deliver physical and digital goods, as well.

One of the powerful ideas that was discovered for rapidly extending the reach of products and services is the network effect. Your product or service becomes more valuable when more people use it. You need to design it in such a way that the growing network adds exponential value for the individual customers.

Facebook, Amazon, Apple and Google have used the network effect to their advantage to become what they are today. Another way to leverage the power of the network effect is by creating appropriate two-sided marketplaces— bringing buyers and sellers together directly and eliminating all the middlemen.

Airbnb and Uber have leveraged this effectively. Engaging customers with Gamification (the application of game-design elements and game principles in non-game contexts) and social media help in effective development of the network effect for individual companies.

Democratized distribution channels help novice entrepreneurs to start a business and quickly compete with established players. Traditional and established companies often miss this revolution that is silently looming in the market, until some start-up suddenly poses serious competition to them. Your job is at risk if you are ignorant of start-up activity in your industry and in your skills set.

3. Birth of new markets

In a capitalist society, consumers have been culturally trained and habituated to consume more and more goods and services. Initially, it was very difficult to change the traditional disposition of humanity from minimalism to consumerism. However, during the post-Great Depression period, the great marketing experts have achieved this phenomenal shift in society. Capitalism thrived for nearly a century after the Great Depression, mainly due to this shift in consumer behavior toward seeking more and even more.

The world has been increasingly accepting new products and services, sometimes for no apparent reason. People just want to try out new things. It has become easier for innovative entrepreneurs to introduce new products and services, and establish them quickly than it has for more established companies.

Chris Anderson calls this phenomenon "The Long Tail." It describes a new market reality where a plethora of products each has a limited number of customers, instead of the earlier scenario where only a few players dominated the entire market.

Before only a handful of companies (with a limited number of products) were serving each industry (the red block in the figure below), but now there are potentially unlimited niches emerging and nimble start-ups have all the infrastructure in place to address those niches. The number of buyers for a given product (popularity) is fewer, but there are so many more products being sold that it greatly extends the overall reach of the marketplace, taken as a whole.

The entire "cake" remains more or less the same size or grows slowly, but it is definitely not growing at the pace of new people entering the party. Before, there were only a few people sharing the cake, but now more people are entering the party and taking a piece of the cake. This reduces the size of the pieces themselves, even though there are more of those smaller pieces, being shared across a greater number of entrepreneurs.

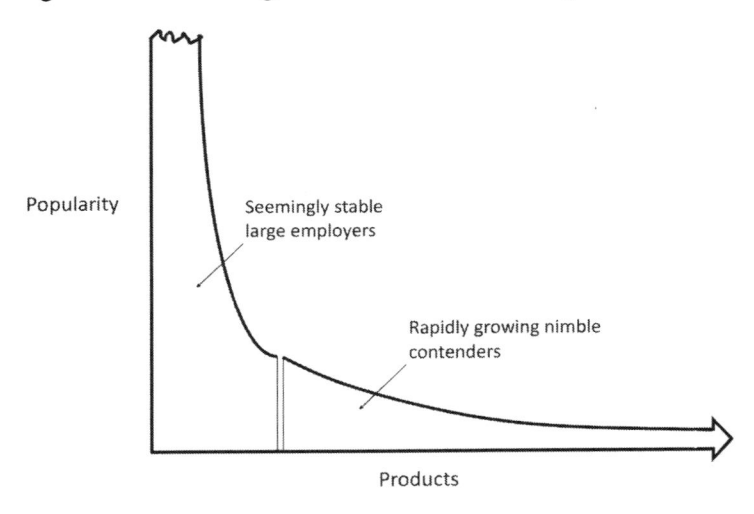

Figure 4. The growing threat to established companies from the new markets

The existing companies are facing a double impact due to this—one from increasing competition and the other from their inability to respond to the market in a timely way, as their start-up counterparts are able to do.

By 2020, it is estimated that nearly 3 billion *more people* will have access to the Internet. For the first time in history, the global marketplace has become accessible to so many more consumers and producers than it ever has before.

The opportunities for collaborative production and distribution is immense. Also for the first time ever, the innovative entrepreneur can access markets on such a scale that they can grow exponentially overnight.

The last decade has witnessed a tremendous boost in entrepreneurship, thanks to these three reasons.

It's time to make your decision

If you think you have a stable job in a medium or large company, you may prove yourself wrong very soon. It all depends on your organization's ability to innovate and compete with the challenging start-ups.

You have two options to choose from:

1. Stay with your long-term employer and risk your job someday.

Business is more volatile today than ever before. There is practically no stable business today. Our perception of stability in our job is limited to the information we have access to. Similarly, the perception of your organization's stability is also limited to the market information *it* has access to.

The Big 3 Technologies are democratizing the way we create and distribute products and services. Because of this, anyone can start a business and challenge even established billion-dollar companies.

We are living in an abundance of information today. It's quite difficult for everyone to diligently choose what they want to read, experience, and act upon in their daily life. There is so much going on out there in the marketplace that it's difficult to sort out in ways that meet one's personal needs.

Budding entrepreneurs are entering into the marketplace and existing stalwarts are entering into bankruptcy, but we are not really able to see all of that because we are deluged by so much information.

The perception of your organization is equally as diminished as yours is, so sticking to a so-called stable job is going to prove disastrous one day.

2. Keep looking for a nimble challenger and switch.

It is possible to move out of your traditional job and join a startup in a fast growing technology, irrespective of your current age, experience, and skills. It's not your skills that are limiting you from finding your dream job. It's actually the application of your skills in the wrong business situation. I am sure you know at least one person who is over-qualified but under-paid and under-recognized in your organization. Many times, you might have also felt the same about yourself.

In fact, feeling that you are over-qualified for a job is good thing. It is telling you to find another, more challenging opportunity, but we often ignore that message, comforting ourselves with the apparent stability we find in our current job.

When things get worse and you no longer stay in your current job (either due to lack of promotion, pay, or whatever reason), you will find it extremely difficult to switch jobs because you have been ignoring the opportunities all along. You will not be able to see what an opportunity looks like.

Spotting the right opportunity is again severely influenced by the deluge of information today. It's quite difficult to find out what *is* an opportunity and what is not, because we are continuously flooded with all sorts of information.

When so much is happening in your own industry and specifically in your profession, unless you keep looking actively for the new entrants into the business and examine their path to success and failure, you will not be able to spot opportunities when you suddenly wake up from your stable job and find out it isn't as stable as you thought it was.

We are talking about taking conscious action in two steps here. First, you need to make up your mind and understand that *there is no stable job in this economy*. The second step is about finding your own career path. This is not an event, but a continuously evolving process.

You need to follow your industry and your profession continuously to understand what success looks like. Only then you can identify the right opportunities for you. Not only that, because you have gone through the journey toward success, you will have the right frame of mind to approach the right stakeholders from your next employer and be able to impress them.

Examine the entrepreneurial activity in your industry. Understand that your profession is evolving in relation to the changing market dynamics and disruptive technologies. Identify how successful people make their choices.

You might not have previously understood that the rising entrepreneurship was a threat to your job, but after you follow this path, you will be able to appreciate both the threat to your stable job and also that there is a cornucopia of opportunities out there.

When you are aware of this game, it's your choice to stick with the stable job until you are over-qualified there or to switch to a challenging new business.

Answer the following questions to stimulate your thinking about your own situation:

1. Are you aware of the start-up activity in your industry? Do you see any threat to your company? If so, how do you mitigate that risk?
2. Check if there are any start-ups trying to make your skills irrelevant by bringing automation to what you do today.
3. Explore if you can help one of those start-ups in accelerating their effort to automation. Who knows? That may become a shortcut for you to become a CEO.

Chapter 5. Millennials Redefine Work

"Life is about making an impact, not making an income."
— Kevin Kruse

Much of what we think about work is based on what was defined during the industrial revolution, including the current way we view working for wages. People went out of their homes and started working for others, primarily to earn their living.

Millennials expect much more than money from their jobs. Millennials have come to terms with their family's expectations and they are much more experimental about their family culture than the corporations and governments are today. They are much more interested in bringing up their children themselves than previous generations were, so they want more time with their family than their forefathers did.

Millennials know that they are going to live beyond 80 years of age and because of this, they also know that they need to work beyond 60 years of age. Most of the millennials work in small companies today and that's where most of the experiments are going on with respect to the way we work.

People want to work whenever they want to, even for a fixed rate and without a guarantee for long-term employment. That's why we see companies like Uber and Upwork thriving.

What do you really expect from your job? Well, it's a complex question. I am sure you want to have at least some of the following:

- A fat pay check (preferably above average among your colleagues)
- Suitable rewards and recognition for your work
- Freedom from micromanagement from your boss, so that you can make independent decisions and move forward

Apart from these, you also definitely need a healthy working environment, with friendly colleagues and management. These expectations have become a norm today, but this was not the case a few generations ago. They just needed a job to survive. For first-generation employees during the industrial revolution, salary was their sole expectation.

We need much more from our jobs than what our parents and grandparents used to expect. What was changed between then and now? From the beginning of the industrial revolution to today, work ethics have been slowly evolving. With millennials entering the workforce, they have undergone a significant facelift.

Multiple surveys worldwide have confirmed that there is a stark difference between the expectations of baby boomers and millennials regarding their jobs.[42]

Out of multiple surveys conducted on happiness, Gallup found that work is the single most important element that defines overall well-being for people in the modern world. Work has never been so much intertwined with the lives of people than today. For millennials, work is much more than a mere job. It defines their personality, social image and, above all, their reason for existence.

Millennials are redefining the ways they seek to meet these expectations, in order to maximize their return from the work. Among the multiple things that they expect from work, the fundamental elements that can cover more than 80% of their expectations are:

1. Money
2. Meaning
3. Freedom

1. Money

Money is one of the fundamental drivers of our motivation to work. Of course, we all need a good pay check at the end of the month. More money can lead to a better quality of life and there is practically no limit to it.

Money as a primal motivation for work is something that has existed ever since humans invented wage-earning work. That's why we have laws on minimum wages that were established all over the industrial world early on.

Just like the price of a product is not dependent on its manufacturing cost, but rather on the perceived value it brings to customers and demand and supply dynamics, wages also behave the same way. A wage is nothing but a price paid by an employer for the services of his/her employee.

We see so many sophisticated products that once ruled the world become irrelevant in the market today. How much do you pay for the first generation of iPhone 2G? Although it was a sensation in 2008, you don't want to buy it today unless you give it some value as an antique.

Our experience and skills also become irrelevant in the marketplace if you do not align to it. Do not expect a salary just because you have a certain number of years of experience or a strong skill set in a particular area. Your worth is decided by the market, based on your relevance to it.

When I was in high school, I was terrified after reading one lesson in social studies. It used to haunt me until I completed my graduation. It was the theory by British economist Thomas Malthus who proposed that the human species is doomed to starvation because of ever-increasing population.

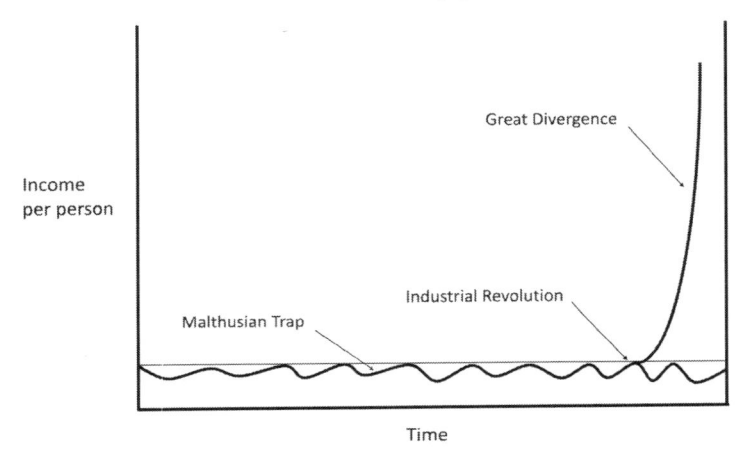

Figure 5: The Malthusian Trap

Based on his study, *The Essay on Principle of Population*, published in 1798, Malthus examined the previous 2000 years of human economic history and proposed that humans would be faced with an inability to produce enough food to feed the growing population.

This was so disappointing to digest, and I used to think that we would run into this situation by the time I reach my adulthood.

Fortunately, Malthus' prediction was wrong. In fact, during the last 200 years, the GDP per capita—a measure of wealth at an individual level—has grown by over 20 times even though the population has only increased by over 5 times. This steep growth in GDP can be explained with the matching growth in technological development.

Not just that, there are no signs of starvation in the near future, either. Rather, we are entering into an age of abundance, not just for food, but for a whole lot more of industrial merchandise and capabilities than we could have ever thought of.

With the industrial revolution, humanity invented wealth creation. As shown in figure 5, we were able to succeed in this journey through continuous innovation leading to increased productivity and wealth.[43] However, the process of wealth creation was sustained mainly because of the quantum leaps in the technology and its application for improving the quality of life.

Established industries can offer stable wealth, but the exponential technologies can offer unlimited leverage for wealth creation. If you are part of it, there is no reason why you can't get a bigger piece of the pie.

The more established a particular skill in the industry is, the less valuable it becomes. Salaries are tightly linked to an individual's experience.

The growth of salaries is mostly mapped to annual inflation. Over the years, the average salary continuously drops for a given amount of experience as skills become established in the market.

We hardly hear about wages growing above industry average in the more traditional industries. Yes, they grow, but only to correct for inflation and to maintain overall living standards in the society.

You may argue that some traditional industries, such as oil and gas, mining, etc. offer above average wages. True, but we also get to see what commands those hefty salaries. In those industries, some people get paid more not because their skills are highly valued, but because they work in hazardous working environments, so it's basically a compensation for the harmful working conditions.

79

On the other hand, think of hi-tech industries or specific roles in traditional industries that need the application of exponential technologies. Their salaries are usually well above the minimum wage, not because the work is hard or the skills are hard to acquire, but because the skills are fresh in the economy and most of the management have no clue how complex the skill really is. Very few people have dared to learn and embrace the unknown territory, so they are paid a premium.

Money is valuable for millennials, but only in the context of their other priorities. As Tim Ferris says in his book, *The 4-hour Workweek*, "Money is multiplied in practical value depending on the number of W's you control in your life: what you do, when you do it, where you do it, and with whom you do it." He calls it a "freedom multiplier."[44] The associated factors of work (i.e. what, when, where, and with whom) are more important to millennials (along with money) because they offer freedom.

Exponential technologies offer more of these Ws, along with more money for comparable experience and skill levels across all industries.

Often it is not previous experience or lack of having necessary skills that limits us in pursuing jobs in these technologies. It's our willingness to accept the unknown, and our tolerance for facing the initial risk, especially when compared to the comfort we all feel in our stable jobs. Once you cross this threshold, you start appreciating the thrill in working on the edge of technologies and the creating of new possibilities in your own industry.

2. Meaning

The minimum wage has potentially addressed the needs of the working population. The significance of earning money from work has been gradually declining, opening up ways to other important elements in life.

Finding a reason for our existence has been a perennial question for humanity. As work occupies most of our waking life, it's obvious that we all try to seek our reason for existence in the work we do.

When you get a decent wage to support your survival and a socially respectful life, the next question you probably think of is the meaning. You might remember Maslow's hierarchy of needs. Of course, it was later proven that these needs are not really hierarchical in nature, but more like being parallel with one another. That means that the hierarchy does not really matter. We seek *all* of those needs all of the time.

Depending on an individual's specific circumstances, the preference for one fundamental need over another keeps changing. It's just that our survival takes priority over other basic needs; we give priority to our biological needs before our psychological needs. When their biological needs are met, people do focus on *any* of the other basic needs (depending on their individual psychological needs at any given time), not necessarily as Maslow's structured them.

The need for finding meaning in our work is one of those fundamental human needs.

Finding meaningful work need not be a complicated thing. There is nothing philosophical about it. We can break it down to simple and tangible things that help us find meaningful work.

Meaningfulness is actually derived from usefulness. The more useful your work is to you and others, the more meaning you derive from it. Our work has no major implications or abstract motives, apart from associating it with some usefulness.

Again, usefulness is not necessarily grand and universal. Of course, the more useful your work is to the maximum number

81

of people, the more meaningful you find it. But it never limits you from feeling meaningful about it, even for the tiniest bit of useful work you do for yourself and especially for others.

We can further break down the usefulness to more mundane results at the workplace. Usefulness is often not directly measured, but you can use the outcomes of usefulness, often reflected from others. They are recognition and reward. When your work is useful, you will get aptly recognized and even rewarded.

That is why there is so much focus on rewards and recognition at mature workplaces in almost all of the industries. Unfortunately, it is attributed to top performance in the workplace. Ideally, it should be given not only to top performers, but to all of those who contributed to the most useful work.

Doing your bit to get your work noticed is as important as finding usefulness in your work. You should not shy away from promoting your work, to let others appreciate it.

It's a competitive world. If you do not promote your work, others may take your credit. It's your responsibility to get your work noticed. When you take care of this, you probably do not miss out on any associated recognition. The recognition is what gives you meaning.

We need to notice an unfortunate phenomenon here. The more established a particular skill is in the industry, the less noticeable it becomes. The output of your work becomes expected and there is nothing spectacular for recognition and reward.

That's why most of the operations-intensive jobs, such as project management and customer support, often go under-appreciated and ill-rewarded, even though they are very challenging.

We see stark differences in pay structure among different skills. Similarly, not all jobs can bring you the same level of recognition and rewards. It does not really depend on the level of skill or salary. The governing rules are different here. Recognition and rewards depend on the perceived usefulness of the output that a particular role brings to the organization.

The exponential technologies score better in this. Because they offer new possibilities and bring in a new sense of hope and enthusiasm, they command higher perceived value within the organization and for its customers. That's why whoever is working in these areas is naturally entitled to more recognition and reward. The nature of the work is not necessarily complicated; the skills needed may not be difficult to acquire. It's just that the outcome of this work qualifies for higher recognition.

I am passionate about personal productivity. I used to write a blog on this initially. With so much effort, I managed to get a few speaking opportunities on this topic. However, when I started speaking about Big Data, I noticed that I could get speaking opportunities much easier than before. It is not because big data as a topic is difficult, but its perceived value is higher in the market.

In fact, I got my first keynote speaking opportunity in a major business conference in Bali, Indonesia, even though I had only spoken three times before on Big Data. I have seen speakers in established areas (such as productivity) still waiting for their first keynote speaking opportunity, even after they had spoken more than 50 times in public forums.

That's the power of exponential technologies. They can offer tremendous opportunities for getting noticed quickly.

3. Freedom

Money and meaning are necessary for an enviable job, but they are not sufficient for a dream job. The third key element that is highly appreciated by millennials is the freedom to work on what one loves to do. Freedom is the choice to express one's ideas freely, the ability to work on what one thinks is meaningful, and also to create value in the way one wants to.

Given a choice, millennials often give more importance to freedom than the other two factors (money and meaning). This was just unthinkable a few hundred years ago.

That's why we see so many organizations shifting to flexible work hours and flat organizational structures. When you have the freedom to decide what to do and how to do things at your workplace, you no longer feel work is an obligatory element in life; rather, you look forward to it. It becomes part of your life.

The industrial revolution has offered jobs that promised job security, but often with an obligatory duty that nobody really wants to do throughout one's lifetime.

Because of the inherent structure and strict line of command in most of the traditional jobs, they were treated like military jobs, where every employee has to obey orders from his/her superior. That limits your creative expression and the need for freedom to do what you think makes sense at your workplace.

With the arrival of the information era in the 20th century, most of the jobs moved towards increasing cognitive skills. "Command" does not work at all times, but rather the mutual discussion and agreement from employees from multiple levels. Teamwork was given priority over one individual dictating the rules.

This slow change over the last century has given enough liberty to the millennials to seek freedom at their workplace, and even to demand it wherever it is lacking.

We often think freedom at the workplace is largely derived from the organizational culture and leadership commitment. Interestingly, there are other elements that also play a major role in the freedom enjoyed by specific roles in any organization. One of them is the nature of the work itself.

The more established a particular role becomes, the less flexible it becomes, leading to an erosion of the freedom of the individual who is taking up that role. Think of a payroll accountant in a finance department. This is something every organization has been doing for centuries.

The only flexibility left to anyone performing this role is to look for changing rules and make better plans for compliance. If you are expecting to exercise free thinking and the ability to come up with your own ways of handling payment processes, this role may not be a good fit for you. Similarly, most of the stable roles (and often most of the roles in established industries) are left with limited freedom for employees to really become creative and express themselves in the workplace.

Exponential technologies win once again. They offer immense freedom of expression, because there are hardly any rules defined in this area. Established companies often have mature processes established as the way they want things done, so employees don't need to experiment. But when companies deal with exponential technologies, their processes are still being developed, so you have more freedom to create your own road to success.

Many people become terribly disappointed with their jobs when they lack one or more of these elements in their jobs. People think of switching their jobs, often seeking just one or two of these three key elements, and eventually become disappointed with their new jobs because they lack the other missing element(s).

Exponential technologies offer more money, meaning, and freedom by the very nature of their evolution. This is not just for millennials. You can get more money, meaning and freedom from your job regardless of your age, especially if you work with these new technologies. It's a choice you need to make today.

In the next Section, I will show you how to find these promising technologies and win the race against the intelligent machines.

Answer the following questions to stimulate your thinking about your own situation:

1. How are salaries growing for your profession? Are they tightly linked to your experience and annual inflation? If so, it's time for you to look for better options.

2. Do you find your work meaningful? Do you receive adequate recognition for your contribution at work? If not, your employer may not be the one to blame for it. Your profession itself can also be the reason for it.

3. Do you have the level of freedom you want to have in accomplishing your work goals?

Section 2
THE SEXIEST JOBS OF THE 21ST CENTURY

Chapter 6. Technologies on the Second Half of the Chess Board

"Technology is a gift of God. After the gift of life, it is perhaps the greatest of God's gifts. It is the mother of civilizations, of arts and of sciences." — Freeman Dyson.

"Any sufficiently advanced technology is indistinguishable from magic." — Arthur C. Clarke

When was the last time you heard about something that was fascinating because it involved advanced technology? Odds are that it was not too long ago. The world is changing so fast! Recent inventions such as smart phones and social networking have become part of our life. Today we can't imagine life without them. Would the thought of a drained phone battery make you stressed?

But the more interesting question is what it means to business when billions of people embrace a particular technology in a matter of a few years. It means an opportunity to create wealth, measured in billions of dollars.

And what does that mean for you and me? A lifetime of opportunity to thrive in that tidal wave of growth.

There is something we need to understand here. When it comes to such a massive rate of change, we just can't grasp it unless we make a conscious effort to put it in the right perspective. Humans are designed to think on a linear scale. We find it easier to notice a gradual change (say, 10% growth per year) and to understand where that growth will lead to if the same growth continues for 10, 20, 30 years more or even beyond. But when things grow on exponential scale (i.e. doubling every time, such as 2x, 4x, 8x, 16x, etc.), it becomes difficult for us to visualize where that ends up after 30 such iterations, for example.

When you walk forward 1 meter and do that 30 times in sequence, you will find yourself 30 meters ahead of your original position. However, if you could double your distance each time and make 30 such attempts, you would have traveled around the Earth 26 times! That is an example of exponential change. Such a rate of change is now observed in some of the technologies.

Today's average smartphone is 1000 times faster and a million times cheaper than the world's biggest supercomputer in the 1970s. This is a classic example of exponential growth.

And a smartphone is not a rare example when it comes to exponential growth. There are multiple other technologies growing at an equal pace. The future is already laid out for those who are busy creating those technologies. Exponential technologies are not intuitive. Knowing about them and adopting them will transform your life and career.

Fortunately for us, there are some clues with which we can sense the next wave of disruption. I spotted one such opportunity, successfully made my career move, and obtained my dream job, even though my background and experience seemed irrelevant for it.

Growth on the Second Half of the Chess Board

Around the 3rd century AD, during the period of the Gupta Empire in India, an unknown genius invented the game of chess and presented it to the Emperor of India. He was one of the very few people back then who understood the power of exponential growth. The king was impressed by the game, so he offered to grant a wish to the inventor. The shrewd inventor asked for a few grains of rice for his survival, but the way he wanted to measure the number of grains was by having one grain in the first square on the chess board and to keep doubling the number of grains in every subsequent square. Looking at his humble wish, the king immediately granted it.

The first few squares contained less than a handful of rice grains. However by the time king's servants filled the squares on the first half on the chess board, they had to offer their entire warehouse full of rice bags. Honoring the promise by completing the full chess board turned out to be an amount of rice equal to the hills of the Himalayas. Then they realized that fulfilling the inventor's wish was beyond the king's capability. When the king fully understood the inventor's wicked plan, I am sure at least one of them got into trouble. While the story says that the inventor was punished for his treacherous motives, the king probably would have understood the power of exponential growth.

The Human Genome Project is a recent example of exponential growth. Begun in 1990, it took 7 years to sequence only 1% of the human genome. Some of the most intelligent people on the planet (such as McKinsey & Company) suggested that the project should be canceled, stating that it was impractical to move forward.

However, the second 1% of work took only one year, and the subsequent work took exponentially less time. In fact, the entire project only took 15 years in total, with 99% of the work only taking about half of the time. Human intelligence could not foresee the power of exponential growth, simply because we are wired to live in a linear, biological world, where things move incrementally.

Exponential technologies often go unnoticed until they reach growth momentum on a par with that of the second half of the chess board. When a billion people start using something in a matter of a few years, it has already changed the world before you even realized it; it has become something people can't live without.

Beginning with the industrial revolution, many exponential technologies that were initially incomprehensible to the general public have changed the social fabric of entire world. The exponential growth of the world GDP is a stark example of this phenomenon.

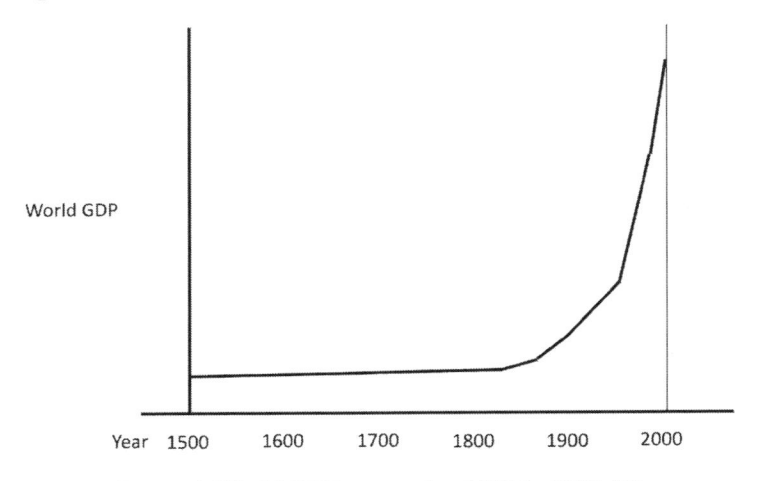

Figure 6: World GDP per capita, 1500 to 2000 AD

World GDP was relatively stable for millennia before taking its leap at the beginning of industrialization. However, as shown in Figure 6, the amount of change was hardly noticeable in the first couple of centuries, but the cumulative effect of the growing economy has changed the world completely from what it used to be a millennium ago.[45]

The cumulative effect from technological progress truly reflects exponential progress. Ray Kurzweil believes that the technological progress in the 21st century will be 1,000 times that of the 20th century.

Many science fiction-like ideas of the 19th century became a reality in the 20th century. Similarly, we don't need to wait for another 1,000 years to realize today's dreams from technology. They are already in the making, much sooner than we think.

Spotting Exponential Technologies in Your Industry

The problem with exponential technologies is that, for many people, they are hard to notice soon enough to gain business benefits before they catch mainstream attention. It would be nice to know when they are in the inception stage and ready to disrupt the market.

So how can you spot the exponential technologies in your industry? Yes, it's difficult to catch them early, but there are certain clues that you can follow to understand and even adopt them. Here are some of the ways to spot exponential technologies early on:

1. Digitalization to Dematerialization

We know that digitalization is an unstoppable phenomenon that is taking place in every industry. Everything is becoming digitalized these days, but only some of these changes affect your job and some may not affect you at all. In many cases, whatever you were doing manually before, you're now doing with the help of computers. When you examine this digitalization carefully, you will see that digitalization is completely eliminating the physical products that we used before. We call this dematerialization.

With dematerialization, you do not need the physical product any more. A software version of it can do everything that a physical product used to do. Think of a music player, radio, calculator, etc. They all got dematerialized with a software version of them plugged into a smartphone. This list is growing rapidly.

The best part of digital products is that they can be replicated into unlimited copies and distributed to anyone for near-zero cost. The exponential growth of digital photos, newspapers, magazines, music, etc. in the recent past is due to the rapid dematerialization of their original physical counterparts. Digitalization leading to dematerialization is a great opportunity for spotting exponential technologies early on. Catching these early in your industry paves the way for you to enter into an emerging industry with practically unlimited potential for growth.

2. De-monetization to Democratization.

Demonetization is removing money out of the game. Does that sound surprising to you? Think of all the free stuff we are enjoying today. We talked about this in Chapter 2. When things become free, their adoption and use grows on an exponential scale, bringing them to practically everyone on the planet. We call this democratization.

Anything free and freely accessible becomes a default choice for anyone who needs it. In the hyper-connected world, anything available for free can be adopted immediately.

When things become democratized, you can find multiple business opportunities along the way, because it opens up new opportunities to reach millions and even billions of potential customers.

In addition, democratization enables people to create new things and share them with others by using freely available means of production and distribution. It further accelerates the process of democratization of the things we need in daily life. We see this already happening in areas such as knowledge, news, art, culture, etc.

You may wonder, if something is available for free, what can I do about it to get my dream job? Look for new businesses being created due to this phenomenon. The successful businesses created using exponential technologies, such as The Big 3 Technologies, have the potential to grow at exponential speed, and so does your career, if you are part of them.

3. Connectivity for Convergence

We know that the world is mostly interconnected and this hyper-connectivity is one of the main reasons behind explosive change in almost every industry. Every change leads to a certain disruption in the way organizations operate. Job seekers' opportunities also get disrupted when businesses change. However, there are certain disruptions that open up a plethora of opportunities for job seekers, among others.

One easy way to spot these opportunities is by observing when connectivity is leading to convergence. When two seemingly different businesses join hands to create value, people think it may fail because it looks irrelevant to the market. However, the growing connectivity creates new platforms and establishes hidden rules that can be uncovered by companies that use this connectivity for convergence of seemingly irrelevant value streams.

Apple, a technology company, has chosen music to be part of their value stream and created a platform for selling music. A new industry was born with this, and millions of people buy music on cloud platforms. But when Steve Jobs made the decision to work with the music industry, people thought it was crazy. Microsoft adopted gaming with Xbox, creating opportunities for millions of game developers and players alike.

Facebook's purchase of the VR Company Oculus Rift may not make much sense today, but it is a perfect example of connectivity leading to convergence. We will see how it opens up opportunities for businesses and job seekers in the next five years.

Uber is quite active in exploiting this trend, exploring convergence opportunities like Uber Eats and UberKittens from a diverse range of businesses.

When I get the question from my students, I usually recommend them to look for such convergence opportunities in The Big 3 Technologies. The upcoming convergence of solar power, energy storage and electric vehicles (EVs) is another sweet spot for dream-job seekers.

Exponential technologies are creating fundamental changes in the economy that will make most of the existing businesses and jobs become irrelevant. Though they are nascent today, I am sure we are going to see them in every industry soon. Hershey's, the largest chocolate manufacturer in North America, has partnered with 3D systems to produce printable food. Look for similar instances in your industry to land your next dream job. A new set of opportunities is emerging for you if you look for them and grab them when you find them.

Answer the following questions to stimulate your thinking about your own situation:

1. What are exponential technologies? How do you spot exponential technologies in your industry?

2. Have you spotted any exponential technologies that pose a threat to your employer? If so, do you have any plan to save your employer?

3. Have you spotted any exponential technologies that pose a threat to your job? If so, can you adopt that technology instead?

4. If you cannot save your job or your employer, what's your way out?

Chapter 7. The Big Three Technologies

There are not more than 5 primary colors, yet in combination they produce more hues than can ever be seen. — Sun Tzu, *The Art of War*

Science fiction authors have already speculated a lot about the technological singularity. You might have read stories or seen movies about machines overtaking humans on physical and mental capabilities, making humans irrelevant on this planet.

Some scientists expect that humans will also evolve into more of transhuman species by injecting AI into their mind and replacing or augmenting various body parts as needed, so you would hardly notice the difference between a machine and a transhuman.

Whatever the outcome will be, today's technology needs to develop three fundamental capabilities in order to reach such a technological singularity.

1. Intelligence beyond what humans can potentially attain
2. Ability to independently communicate with other machines
3. Ability to create new things

When machines can attain these three capabilities, it's just a question of time before we need to worry about singularity. I see that the seeds for these three capabilities were planted in the Big 3 Technologies.

1. Artificial Intelligence (AI): It is expected to surpass the combined intelligence of the entirety of humanity by the end of next decade[46]
2. Internet of Things (IoT): The number of connected devices has already surpassed the human population. When robots get AI and are connected to one another, they can move and act much like humans do.
3. 3D Printing: It is currently at the nascent stage, but definitely on the disruption curve. The so-called singularity will become a reality when intelligent machines can access 3D printing machines and print whatever they want.

It still looks like science fiction, but the seeds are real and progress is evident. The combined effect of these three technologies can bring the technological singularity to our world sooner than we think. That's why I call them The Big 3 Technologies.

Of course, we need multiple other disruptive technologies like robotics, solar energy harvesting, etc. to complete this mission. But the fundamental capabilities brought by The Big 3 Technologies need to evolve first, irrespective of the maturity of other disruptive technologies.

The Big 3 Technologies will play a vital role in our business and professional life. We need to understand how these technologies are changing the business and job market. Let's see how they are developing and impacting the job market.

Artificial Intelligence (AI)

During the last 50 years, we have seen computers taking over most of the manual work and doing it better, cheaper and faster. When a computer performs a mathematical operation to solve a simple addition problem or provides search results based on a keyword, it is actually executing a pre-written program, which takes inputs and gives output in a predefined format.

But this is changing now. The programs are becoming intelligent to the extent that they can learn and act independently in new situations. We call this ability Artificial Intelligence (AI). It has been growing exponentially during the last 5 years.

The immediate applicability for AI lies in taking over high-paying jobs that involve complex but repetitive mental tasks, like those you find in jobs such as business analysts, financial brokers and certain software developers.

Some of the leading technology company CEOs have declared that the 21st century is the era of AI.

IBM's Watson supercomputer had already demonstrated what is possible with AI five years ago. In 2016, IBM CEO Ginni Rometty said, "I would say in five years, there's no doubt in my mind that cognitive AI will impact every decision made, from health care to education to financial services." Amazon CEO Jeff Bezos thinks that AI will have a profound impact on society over the next 20 years. He says, "It's really early but I think we're on the edge of a golden era. It's going to be so exciting to see what happens."[47]

Larry Page describes his vision for Google search as an embedded intelligence in people's brains. When you think about something you don't know much about, you will automatically get the information from embedded intelligence. The AI needed to make it possible is coming to maturity in the next couple of decades. Google CEO Sundar Pichai said AI will be an integral part of everything Google is going to develop. He hopes that Google will be your AI friend.[48]

While the future is still difficult to imagine, you cannot ignore the forecasts of these major influencers, especially when you see the present capabilities of AI.

In the 5 years since 2011, when it won the *Jeopardy* game show, IBM's Watson has improved a whopping 2,400%. Google's voice recognition technology now claims 98% accuracy. Facebook's DeepFace is believed to recognize faces with a 97% success rate.[49]

The maturity of AI is measured by the Turing test, developed by Alan Turing in 1950. It is a method of determining whether or not a computer is capable of thinking like a human. AI is said to have cleared the Turing test when a human is unable to distinguish it from another human being by using the replies to questions put to both.

Over the last 60 years, scientists have been working hard to build an AI that could pass the Turing test. Although AI may not pass the Turing test for general purposes anytime soon, some of the existing AI programs have already passed the Turing test in controlled environments.

The Georgia Institute of Technology in the USA offers an online course in AI. In 2016, about 300 students registered for this course and were assisted by a Teaching Assistant called Jill Watson. At the end of the course, the students were shocked to find out that Jill was actually a bot, powered by the IBM Watson platform. "It seemed very much like a normal conversation with a human being," one student said. "I was flabbergasted," confessed another[50]. We are on the verge of an AI revolution today. Given the exponential nature of this technology, you shouldn't be surprised to see AI clearing such tests in multiple other areas of our daily life in the next 5 years. The Big 3 Technologies and their convergence will eventually take us closer to the technological singularity. They are the technologies that will help you transform your career.

Just like electricity has created so many animated objects during the past century, AI is going to create intelligent objects in the 21st century. Everything that was formerly electrified will now be cognitized.

This so-called intelligence is not limited to objects, but will augment us *individually* by deepening our memory and speeding our recognition, and *collectively* as a species. Electricity has transformed almost all of the daily objects we use and also created a plethora of new objects to make our life more comfortable and to create new possibilities. All those objects can now be made new, different, or more interesting by infusing them with some extra intelligence.

AI is going to be one of the biggest entrepreneur opportunities for the 21st century and it's already here. Kevin Kelly says that if you want to start a company, it's easy to come up with an idea: Take X and add AI.[51]

While AI is increasingly being chosen by budding entrepreneurs, its capacities and general applications are being extended further by the scientific community, at a feverish pace.

Scientists at Insilico Medicine have developed a new drug-discovery engine that is capable of predicting therapeutic use, toxicity, and adverse effects of thousands of molecules, advancing the laborious drug-discovery process[52].

MIT has developed AI algorithms that can produce realistic sounds. These sounds are so natural that even humans got fooled by them. Such a capability helps robots be aware of their surroundings and act accordingly.[53]

It won't be long until it will feel completely natural for us to consult an artificial "hive mind" when making important decisions. You will feel more confident following the suggestions of AI rather than depending on your best friends, colleagues or even mentors.

A swarm of lots of minds working together is better at predicting the outcome of something than any single person would be. In June 2016, an artificial hive mind called UNU was answering questions from participants in an "Ask Me Anything" session on Reddit.com, using its swarm intelligence. Since its 2014 inception, this AI system has correctly predicted Oscar winners and Super Bowl winners, outperforming human experts in the process. You can also play around with it here: http://go.unu.ai/

Cars are the first consumer robots powered by AI

AI-powered self-driving cars are not meant for the fancy or luxury market. They are getting safer and cheaper even before they hit the consumer markets. Even in their early stages, they have already proved to be significantly safer and more efficient than human-driven cars, creating another trillion-dollar market and disrupting the existing automobile industry.

In October 2015, Tesla wirelessly released a software update that gives self-driving functionality to its cars. Because of its already-existing customer base, Tesla now gathers more data from its autopilot system in a single day than what Google has been gathering since 2009 from Google's autonomous driving program. The autopilot system is improving steadily from the growing field data, as Tesla is collecting more data from its growing customer base.

Following the release of his autopilot system, Elon Musk made a bold safety claim about Tesla's Autopilot function: "The probability of having an accident is 50% lower if you have Autopilot on. Even with our first version."[54]

The self-driving car is not the privilege of elite companies like Google and Tesla anymore. The technology has already been democratized to the extent that more flexible and modular versions are available to apply to any car and make it into a self-driving car within a few hours.

Dr. Roshy John, head of the Robotics and Cognitive Systems Department of Tata Consultancy Services, along with his team of engineers, has created a self-driving Tata Nano that's tailored to thrive in India's traffic and roads. Dr. John also created a modular version of the system that turns any car into an autonomous one in less than an hour.[55]

Otto, a start-up founded by ex-Google employees, has created a kit to retrofit a commercial truck and turn it into a self-driving truck. Otto has successfully tested their sensor-laden hardware and OS in transforming a Volvo VNL 780 into a self-driving truck.[56] Thanks to Otto's kits, fleet-management companies can create their own self-driving fleets without replacing every single vehicle.

The self-driving car is possibly the first consumer product that combines robotics and AI in action. It poses a serious threat to millions of cab drivers and other professional drivers.

Health Care

We trust doctors so much that we do not even think of going anywhere except to a doctor when we get ill. Do you know that medical errors in hospitals are the third leading cause of death in the U.S., after heart disease and cancer?

Despite this fact, if we cannot avoid going to a doctor, do we have a choice? Until recently, the answer was "no," but now it is changing to "yes." AI is coming to our rescue. Data-driven diagnoses and treatment plans are transforming the health care industry.

Using AI, UCLA scientists have made significant progress in cancer diagnosis. They created a device that images cancer cells (without destroying them) and identifies 16 physical characteristics. The main component of this device is a photonic time-stretch microscope coupled with a powerful deep-learning algorithm that can analyze 36 million images per second and spot cancer cells with 95 percent accuracy.[57]

AI is making rapid progress in diagnosis and identifying customized treatment plans. I see that health care is currently undergoing disruption with AI and it will be democratized soon.

Creative Arts

AI can already produce music and help creative artists with fresh ideas to inspire them.

Sunspring is a short sci-fi film, written and composed entirely by an AI called Benjamin. Ars Technica, a technology news and information website that exclusively debuted *Sunspring*, describes the unusual creative process that was used to train Benjamin with dozens of '80s and '90s sci-fi screenplays and some 30,000 pop songs for the musical interlude. *Sunspring* placed in the top 10 in the Sci-Fi London contest, beating out hundreds of other entries[58].

Google aims to build an artists' community around machine-generated art, so it came up with a similar AI program called Magenta, built on top of the open-source TensorFlow system. Magenta helps musicians and artists compose creative music as part of their natural creation process.[59]

Law

Practicing law involves crunching loads of documents and case histories. AI is well positioned to outsmart humans in this area. A survey from the Law Society's Robots and Lawyers conference found that 48% of respondents' firms already use some form of artificial intelligence (AI) and 4% of the respondents already agreed that lawyers will eventually be replaced by robots.[60]

Remember ROSS, which I mentioned in the first chapter. AI lawyers are already in the market and competing for jobs along with human lawyers. You know how exponential growth works. How much time do you think it will take for AI lawyers to flood the market and replace human lawyers?

Chatbots

Virtual assistants and chatbots are ready to serve businesses with simple tasks such as scheduling events, answering simple questions related to products, services, processes, etc. They have already matured enough to replace the majority of the customer service agents.

Personal assistants are no longer for those sitting in the corner office. Practically every employee can have access to assistants that are much more efficient than a human personal assistant. They assist employees with questions like, "What's the password to the office Wi-Fi network?", "Who's in charge of sales in the London office?" etc.

It was estimated in a study that employees spend about 20% of their time looking for information, or looking for a person who has the information they need[61]. Chatbots can save that time for employees.

AI-powered assistants are entering into the customer service roles for airlines, hotels, banks and many other businesses.

We already see how Siri, Cortana, and Alexa are helping individual users and providing increasingly popular personal assistants. There is also growing list of AI-powered mobile apps. For example, EasilyDo and 24Me are free apps that can do very intuitive and powerful cognitive tasks for you. They are definitely more efficient and above all, they are free. Do you still want to use a human personal assistant for these tasks?

In the next 3 to 5 years, AI is expected to reach new heights in the following areas:

1. AI applications will pass the Turing Test.
2. All 5 human senses will be part of the computing experience.
3. AI can help us solve some of the biggest challenges, such as terrorism and climate change.
4. AI can be humanity's best doctor.
5. AI will be part of our daily lives, both physically and virtually.

AI technology is well positioned to disrupt industries, grow on an exponential scale and displace millions of jobs. Every employee needs to be aware of its impact and plan his/her career accordingly.

The Internet of Things (IoT)

The planet has grown a central nervous system and that is called the Internet of Things (IoT). While AI is eliminating jobs, IoT is creating jobs, at least in the short term.

This is because the whole world is getting smarter, thanks to IoT. Industry trends such as Smart Cities, Smart Homes, Smart Grid, Smart Factories (also known as Industry 4.0) are opening up multi-trillion-dollar business opportunities. No industry and profession can possibly escape this revolution. You either become part of this revolution or become irrelevant in the oncoming smart world.

IoT is considered to be the biggest technology revolution after the industrial revolution. Its economic impact is around

20% of the GDP of the entire world. Today it is economically feasible to generate data from every living and non-living *thing*, connect it to the global internet network, monitor, control, and intercommunicate with other connected things. This capability is enabling us to find applications beyond our reach a few decades ago.

While connectivity and intelligence improve, multiple things can interact with one another and perform tasks without human involvement. Imagine the world with IoT in action.

Automobiles, electrical appliances, from animate to inanimate things–practically every *thing* that is important to us—will be connected through a gargantuan network of sensors, each connected with its own IP address. Each can talk to other things and to humans, each can potentially influence the functioning of other things, making our life truly dramatic.

Your smartphone can help you find your car keys. Nothing gets lost because everything gets tracked. Your appliances can reorder consumables such as groceries, cleaning products, and whatever you use, without your intervention.

Companies will be able to make things in quantities that are just sufficient for your needs, by sourcing only the necessary raw materials, streamlining supply chains and minimizing waste to an extraordinary degree. The productivity and efficiency of organizations can be improved to achieve a near-zero marginal cost of producing them. Individuals can expect cheaper goods and services (and some of them even available for free), in addition to improved convenience in daily life.

The World Economic Forum forecasts that, by 2022, one trillion sensors will be connected to the internet. By 2024, with thousands of sensors per human being on the planet, more than 50% of internet traffic will be delivered to homes for appliances and devices.[62]

We need to redesign all the devices we use in daily life to be "digitally connectable," so that they can perceive their environment comprehensively and act autonomously—a daunting task that could potentially turn every company into a software company.

The IoT revolution is primarily triggered by the falling prices of sensors, ubiquitous connectivity, and the growing adoption of cloud computing. Businesses that are required to monitor their physical assets, organizational processes and understand what's happening with their customers are ready to adopt IoT technology.

Individuals can monitor their homes, pets, kids and practically whatever they need to. The technology is so promising that the question now is not about whether you need it or not, but how you can take advantage of this.

You shouldn't be surprised if nations build a dedicated network for IoT. It is inevitable. In fact, the Netherlands has become the first country to create a dedicated network for IoT. As of June 2016, about 1.5 million objects from various businesses, utilities and private users were connected to this network.[63]

The biggest benefit of IoT comes from bridging the gap between the analog world (machines, things, people, animals, plants, etc.) and the digital world. With this, digital capabilities such as the speed of light and easy integration with other systems can be passed on to our analog world. IoT comes as a savior to the automation-impacted job market.

3D Printing

"Three-dimensional printing makes it as cheap to create single items as it is to produce thousands and thus undermines economies of scale. It may have as profound an impact on the world as the coming of the factory did... . Just as nobody could

have predicted the impact of the steam engine in 1750—or the printing press in 1450, or the transistor in 1950—it is impossible to foresee the long-term impact of 3D printing. But the technology is coming, and it is likely to disrupt every field it touches. — The Economist, February 10, 2011 print edition.

Compared to AI and IoT, 3D printing (the third of The Big 3 Technologies) may take some more time to disrupt the job market, but its potential is equally immense. It is a revolutionary technology that bridges the gap between the digital and physical worlds.

Historically, we manufactured material objects by casting, fabrication, stamping and machining processes. All of these processes *eliminate* the *unnecessary* material from a block of raw material, so that the desired object is made. In the 1980s, scientists developed some tools and processes to build objects by *adding* material layer by layer, and called it Additive Manufacturing (AM).

During the last decade, the technology has advanced to an extent that the additive manufacturing process was boxed into a single machine that can take raw material and produce a 3D object by reading the design of the object completely from a software program, just like printing text from a computer. We call this 3D printing because it is now possible to create a physical object directly from a digital copy, with no human intervention needed during the process of printing.

3D printing is expected to become a household tool that anyone can use to print household objects instead of purchasing them from a store. For example, if you need objects like a measuring cup or a flower pot, you can print them if you have a 3D printer at home.

A research report released by PwC in April 2016 stated that over two-thirds of US manufacturers are already using 3D printing (primarily for prototyping), and the leading barrier to even greater adoption is the lack of talent.[64]

3D printing helps us innovate faster by allowing people to move from the abstract *idea* to building physical objects that you can touch and feel. Ideas often have flaws that you may not realize until the last stage—until you actually build the real products.

With 3D printing, you can create the prototype quickly so that you can validate your ideas before investing in full-scale production. In fact, it teaches us that failure is indeed a necessary part of our process. As Mark Zuckerberg says, "Fail fast and fail forward." We can effectively implement this in the product innovation development process by using 3D printing.

The complexity of the objects being manufactured using 3D printing technology is growing at an exponential rate. By March 2015, Boeing was using around 300 different 3D-printed aircraft production parts in 10 different aircraft production programs.[65] Airbus introduced Thor, the world's first 3D-printed aircraft at the International Aerospace Exhibition 2016 in Schoenefeld, Germany. This 13-feet-long windowless drone (with a weight of 46 pounds) shows us the future of manufacturing.

3D printing eliminates most of the manual processes such as initial setup, preparing molds, etc., saving significant time and effort when compared to traditional manufacturing. With 3D printing, all you need is the design in the soft copy and raw material with which to print.

3D printing is not limited to material objects. 3D printing has been rapidly making inroads to alternate forms of manufacturing such as the biotechnology and food processing industries. In fact, food printing is growing rapidly these days and it is going to disrupt the entire food-processing as well as restaurant industries. 3D printing is the best option for printing synthetic body parts because of its ability to print a unique design for just one person without affecting the cost.

Imagine what's going to happen to the decorative arts industry. Practically all the graphic visualizations we see on a screen can be potentially materialized and objectified. We could touch and feel those pieces of art that are currently limited to only the screen. In producing pieces of art using 3D printing, your creativity and imagination are the only real limit.

Education and learning are going to be transformed with 3D printing. We no longer need to imagine things. We can print complex objects, use them for teaching and learning purposes and then remodel them into completely different objects for the next class.

Researchers at Cornell University developed the On-the-Fly-Print system that allows a designer to develop 3D models in CAD, while simultaneously printing them. Explaining this system, Kurzweil reports in his blog that the interactive prototyping approach enables designers to "pause anywhere in the process to test or measure and make needed changes, which will be added to the physical model [that is] still in the printer."

3D printing has entered into some serious business, as well. It is no longer limited to printing toys or funny human faces.

The government of Dubai has shown the maturity of this technology by building the world's first 3D-printed office that will form the home of the Dubai Future Foundation. It only took 18 people, working for just 17 days, to complete the fully functional 250-square-meter office building, which had running water, electricity and air conditioning. The efficiency improvement demonstrated by this project justifies the promise of 3D printing. Compared to the traditional construction project, it reduced the waste by up to 60%, cut production time by up to 70%, and reduced labor costs by as much as 80%.[66]

Inexpensive consumer 3D printers are already on their way to our shopping malls. San Francisco-based OLO 3D Inc. is one such company active in this market. OLO claims that their $99 device enables users to print 3D objects as thick as 1-inch of material in just under 2 hours straight from their smartphones. OLO's new Kickstarter campaign has raised more than $2 million in 2016.

We've seen how a variety of physical devices have been dematerialized into smartphone apps, and now OLO is working hard to dematerialize and demonetize the traditional manufacturing process, in order to democratize 3D manufacturing by bringing it to anyone with a touchscreen smartphone. Ultimately 3D printing can dematerialize, demonetize and democratize the manufacturing industry and turn everyone into a creator.

Convergence of The Big 3 Technologies

We get to see the magical effect of these technologies when they are combined to solve some of the toughest problems of humanity. Any device that is connected will become "smart" because it can tap into the AI in the cloud. Things that are not connected will become increasingly "dumb" and eventually become irrelevant in our life. On the other hand, intelligent things can communicate with one another and eventually with creative machines like 3D printers to produce new intelligent machines.

Convergence enables unparalleled, customized experiences for humanity. Convergence of The Big 3 Technologies on such a broader scale is still in a very nascent stage, but we are certainly moving in that direction.

When IoT is combined with AI, intelligence becomes ubiquitous. For example, we have smart apparel today for a variety of purposes. Shirts that act as smart-phone antennas, workout clothes that monitor one's fitness level, sports equipment that monitors performance, a bandage that tells your doctor how well the tissue beneath it is healing, or a flexible fabric cap that senses brain signals—all these things are already technically feasible and budding entrepreneurs are working hard to make them available to consumers.

AI powerhouses join hands with network majors to harness the combined effect of AI and IoT. In June 2016, IBM announced a partnership with Cisco to take their Watson out of the cloud and put it closer to the machines. Running Cisco's gateway gear, Watson has got a new task: to predict the behavior of machines that are not even connected to the Internet. High-speed boat maker SilverHook Powerboats is running Watson on their boats to make sure the engines are running smoothly, as they reach speeds of up to 200 miles per hour.[67]

Local Motors, a crowd-sourced car-design platform and creator of the world's first 3D-printed car, has developed the first self-driving "cognitive" vehicle, another example of the power of converging exponential technologies—in this case, AI, sensors and robotics.

This 12-passenger vehicle, dubbed Olli, uses IBM's new Watson Internet of Things system to process data from 30+ sensors in the vehicle and enable passengers to interact with the vehicle using natural language. Olli behaves so much like a human that it can even discuss topics such as how the vehicle works, where they are going, and why it is making specific driving decisions. And the best part is that, because Local Motors will produce the car in its micro factories, they're able to make performance tweaks and other improvements every time they build a new Olli vehicle.

3DPrintler, a start-up launched in 2015, added the power of AI to 3D printing. They built a chatbot that helps users to search, compare and order 3D prints from nearby 3D print service providers. Ordering 3D prints is currently a time-consuming and slightly boring process. An intelligent bot is a perfect solution to patiently take users through the different steps. The company has witnessed a big jump in sales with the chatbot compared to their sales from the website.[68]

The Big 3 Technologies are going to bring abundance to our world beyond our imagination. They emancipate humanity from physical and mental work, but unfortunately will be taking away millions of jobs along the way. Ironically, they are the harbingers of dream jobs, too.

Irrespective of what industry you are in and what your role is, you can find relevance for these technologies in your work, so you can create new possibilities for your business or for your employer. It's in the very process of building new capabilities and solving the existing problems in better ways that you find your dream job, more money, meaning, and freedom.

You need to understand what skills, mindset and attitudes will help in navigating these technologies and challenging times ahead. In the subsequent chapters, I try to answer these questions.

Answer the following questions to stimulate your thinking about your own situation:

1. Why do you need to monitor and understand The Big 3 Technologies?
2. How does Artificial Intelligence impact your industry? How do you save your job from it?
3. What opportunities do you see in your industry and especially for your career from the growing implementation of IoT solutions?

4. Why do you think 3D printing is one of the fundamental capabilities in the journey to the technological singularity? Can you find any opportunities to participate in that journey?

5. How does the convergence of The Big 3 Technologies transform your industry? What can you do about it?

Chapter 8. You Are Not an Outsider to the Party

"One machine can do the work of fifty ordinary men. No machine can do the work of one extraordinary man."
— Elbert Hubbard

If you are working in the tech world, you should be working in any of these three areas unless you are on the bench (common term in the IT industry for having no assigned work):

1. Technical solution development: software engineers, solution architects, and all those working on the code, either directly or indirectly

2. Direct business support: sales, marketing, HR, finance, procurement and the like

3. Indirect business support (all those who support the above two classes of people): business analysts, project managers, and all those who do not directly add value that is delivered directly to the customer.

Even for industries other than information technology, this classification should hold good. You either create value directly, or support those who create value in different functional areas (such as HR, finance, sales & marketing, etc.), which are fundamentally same across all industries, or you are nobody, with a so-called fancy title.

The general perception is that only the technical developers can expect to get into exponential technologies, if they can get a chance to work on them. I see that some people think it's very difficult for those working in any of the supporting roles to enter into disruptive technologies. It is simply not true. In fact, it is easier for *non-technical* people to enter into any of the disruptive technologies, because you don't necessarily need to have the prior technical expertise.

Finding a way to enter into a promising technology is one of the main things you have to figure out in pursuit of your dream job. The relevance of your experience, skills and knowledge are some of the direct indicators of your eligibility for any job. In that sense, relevance is apparent and vividly defined for all technical roles.

For all non-technical roles, this relevance is loosely defined. If you are in a business support role, your so-called experience, skills and knowledge are also still relevant for any business in disruptive technology. However, the scale and quality of their relevance may vary.

If you are a software engineer, either you have worked on Java or not. That's it. You can't really find a place that is partially true for that skill.

However, if you are a marketing manager for a financial services company, you can transfer the relevance of your marketing experience to other companies that are working on disruptive technologies, such as IoT or AI.

The people belonging to the third group (indirect business support) may often find it very hard to switch their jobs because they find it difficult to associate themselves with any technology or product that drives value in the industry they are seeking to become part of. These so-called generalists do not realize the damage they are inflicting on their careers when they keep themselves away from the activities that directly create value.

It is possible to get your dream job in emerging technologies, irrespective of your age, experience and skill set. However, you may have mental barriers that are keeping you from pursuing your dream job, based on incorrect assumptions you have made about what is required.

Mapping Your Experience to Any of The Big 3 Technologies

I know how frustrating it is to be part of something that does not add value to a business. I was one of them. My search for my dream job helped me find better avenues for generalists who want to find their dream jobs.

In fact, the more seemingly irrelevant to a business you are, the easier it is to create your own identity, especially for venturing into disruptive technologies. Let's see how that works.

Irrespective of your current industry and role, ask yourself the questions in the table below to get ideas on:

- What business problems to focus on
- Which technology to choose for your dream job
- How to manage the expectations of those who can potentially hire you, etc.

What You Do is similar to	Your Current Role sounds like	Ask this question to identify an opportunity	Ask this question to find an idea	Ask this question to make it happen
Developers (those who directly create value for their customers)	Software Engineer, Systems Architect, Designer, Data Scientist, etc.	What disruptive technologies are built on the technical skills I already have or those I can learn quickly?	What can I build to create massive value to the industry?	Who needs to be convinced about my idea and how can I prove its worth?
Direct Business Support (those who support developers)	Functional expert in HR, Finance, Supply Chain, Procurement, Sales & Marketing, etc.	What new possibilities is my business function going to have? (look into other industries to get inspiration)	Using any of these technology capabilities, what's one thing that I can improve in my current business?	Who needs to be convinced about my idea and how can I prove its worth?
Indirect Business Support (those who does not fall into the above two categories)	Business Analyst, Project Manager, Pre-sales, Research Analyst, etc.	How can I move out of this role? What can I learn quickly to build expertise, either in a technology or an industry or both?	Read and talk to experts. Then ask yourself, "What is one techno-functional area in which I can build further expertise?	Who needs to be convinced about my idea and how can I prove its worth?

This exercise may not enable you to land your dream job right away, but it certainly helps you understand that, irrespective of your background, you can switch to a career in any exponential technology.

Employers and Employees Are Two Different Species

The key challenge for entrepreneurs who want to start a business in disruptive technologies is the technological complexity and even the lack of economic feasibility for the identified use. Because of the lack of standardization and viable architectures, entrepreneurs are not able to invest in the seemingly utopian applications.

On the other hand, job seekers have a completely different perspective and expectations, which do not often match what the entrepreneurs are looking for. There is an excitement and hype in the industry that gives rise to exaggerated hopes for job seekers.

In addition to this, job seekers also suffer lack of clarity on how they can become qualified for what they seek. This combination of exuberance and lack of clarity keeps them oscillating between hope and despair.

The entrepreneur's challenges can become opportunities for aspiring employees who can understand those challenges. This is more relevant and intense for disruptive technologies because entrepreneurs lack experience and there is no historical reference to fall back upon for their entire journey to success. The entry barriers are flexible and less intense for almost all skills in these businesses.

All you need is a compelling idea and the confidence to demonstrate its feasibility. Depending on the nature of the work, you might have to show some technical skills and proof of concepts at times, but the need for a plausible idea and strong confidence in that idea can't be overstated.

John, a friend of mine, has started his career in sales in the communications industry. He understood early on that the communications industry is embracing IoT at the speed of light. He made strategic steps to understand the game of selling IoT based products and solutions and successfully moved into a leading IoT platform company as a regional director. From practically zero experience in IoT to a regional director. That's a pretty impressive journey!

Another friend of mine, Vijay, has started his career as an SAP consultant in an IT company, working initially for utility companies. He saw the massive career growth prospects with exponential technologies when combined with domain expertise. He quickly learned IoT technology principles and started writing about applying them for the utility industry. His thought leadership eventually reached multiple influencers, who pulled him up in his career by offering valuable opportunities. He is now running multiple industry initiatives on promoting IoT in the utility industry, apart from working full-time as an IoT architect, all starting from being an SAP consultant.

As a job seeker, you know that these are promising opportunities. You may feel that you are not qualified for them because you don't know these technologies. We need to realize that the technology is only one part of the business, and all other aspects (such as identifying the business need, evaluating the cost/benefit, and sourcing all the necessary resources for building the business—even the entire game of sales and marketing) remain more or less the same for any technology business.

As long as you are in business, you can find your relevance in most of today's disruptive technologies. You can become qualified for your dream job in most of the disruptive technologies, often quicker and easier than you think.

It's easier because you don't need to gain years of experience. Nobody can have decades of experience in a budding technology. It's also easier because you don't need to learn new skills. I know that sounds totally counterintuitive: How can I get the job without having the right skills?

A skill is the demonstrated ability to do a certain task. As the technology is new and the possibilities have not yet been explored, you probably don't have the right skills, but that does not stop you from seeking a job in this field. To secure your dream job in this field, you just need the right idea and the right frame of mind to solve the problem, rather than the demonstrated skill.

Of course, you should have enough *relevant* experience in your traditional background. For example, if you are seeking your dream job in IoT solutions marketing, you should have been already working as a marketing manager in some other business. But just because you did not market IoT solutions, you don't need to think you are not eligible for it.

Irrespective of your current role, you can find your dream job in emerging technologies if you can adopt the right mindset. I'll talk about what that mindset is in the next chapter.

Answer the following questions to stimulate your thinking about your own situation:

1. What role do you play in your organization? Do you create value directly or do you support those who create direct value? You are in danger if you don't belong to either of these roles.

2. In case you are not in a role that adds value to the customer directly, find a disruptive technology and aim to find a job that *does* add value directly.

3. If you create value directly for your customer in your current job, what disruptive technologies can you learn quickly?

Chapter 9. Winning the Race against Machines

"If no mistake have you made, yet losing you are...a different game you should play." — Yoda

"But they are useless. They can only give you answers."
— Pablo Picasso, on computers.

If you are still doing the same work that is elsewhere being done by a machine, forget about expecting higher wages inside or outside of your organization. Every job that *can* be automated *will be* automated. Every job that *can* be outsourced *will be* outsourced, eventually. No business or government can stop this trend.

Your job is going to be taken up by machines, at least partially. It may happen sooner than you think if your current job requires that you perform the same set of tasks, step-by-step, over and over again. A predefined repeatable work is also known as algorithemic work because it can be easily automated with an algorithm. It does not matter whether your job involves manual tasks or mental tasks or a combination of both.

This is already happening, not just in the technology industry, but in every industry. Every exponential technology finds its application in every industry. It is just a question of time as to when a particular industry will adopt them.

In the coming decade, The Big 3 Technologies are going to find their place in almost all industries. Whether you are in hospitality, marketing, HR, supply chain management or in shop floor production management, you will be impacted by these technologies, and it is the time for you to save your job.

What job can you expect in this situation? You can't escape from this into a different world. In fact, the whole world is now pretty much the same. Globalization has connected the whole world and thoroughly changed the workplace with a uniform code of conduct. Other companies are not so different from yours. Employees in other companies face the same troubles as you do. When everything is automated, everything we do is taken up by machines. Do we really have anything left to do?

In his book *Only Humans Need Apply*, author Thomas Davenport proposes an approach to save jobs from automation by building skills, looking at all sides and finding areas where machines can't reach your skill.[69] He suggests that you can:

- Step Up: Find jobs that involve higher-level decision-making, such that computers can't possibly make such decisions as part of what needs to be automated.

- Step Aside: Find jobs that demand skills a computer cannot perform, at least for now.

- Step In: Find jobs that focus on improving the decisions made by computers.

- Step Narrowly: Find a niche and build your skills strongly enough that investing in automation does not make economic sense.

- Step Forward: Build skills to develop new systems and technology that support intelligent decisions and actions.

It is a good strategy to escape automation. It helps you to find alternate ways to dodge automation and find a job you can depend on, at least for some time.

However, there are some limitations with this approach. Most of these strategies are only suitable for those who have technical skills. For example, if you are an accountant and your current job is being automated, you may find it difficult to choose any of those strategies. Also, this model does not help you find your dream job; forget about finding ways to thrive in the second machine age through using these strategies.

Winning the Race against Machines

When a factory worker is trying to operate a machine along with a robot next to him, he's trying to race against the machine. When a knowledge worker is trying to translate a piece of text from language A to language B, alongside a translator on a computer, he's trying to race against the machine. When a data scientist is trying to build an algorithm alongside a self-learning algorithm, he's trying to race against the machine.

This is a one-sided game. Racing against the machines has a clear outcome. There is only one option left to humans. To lose.

It's time for us to identify our role in the second machine age. As what we have been doing historically is increasingly being done by machines, the role of humans in the 21st century and beyond is becoming increasingly complimentary to what intelligent machines do.

Instead of racing AGAINST the machine, race WITH the machine.

Racing *against* the machine is doing what machines are already doing elsewhere and expecting a secure and promising job.

Racing *with* the machine is creating value for your organization by:

- Identifying new possibilities, communicating your ideas and solving existing problems better, faster and cheaper, utilizing the power of machines;
- Solving new problems that nobody thought could be solved; and
- Doing what machines cannot do on their own.

The secret to winning the race against machines is *teaming* with machines, racing *with* them rather than racing *against* them.

Just like we all have limitations, machines also have limitations, at least for the next few generations. Because of such limitations, machines cannot accomplish tasks as we want them to be handled.

Artificial intelligence and the so-called intelligent robots are typically built to accomplish specific niche tasks. Usually they can't either think or act outside of their particular scope, although this scope has been getting broader over the years. So we still need to complement the machines with those missing skills.

In fact, these skills can be very well supplied by humans. When Gary Kasparov was defeated by IBM's Deep Blue in 1997, people thought we had come to an end of human intelligence in playing chess. However, when Gary tested playing chess with the help of *another* computer, he could consistently defeat the first machine.

In multiple industries, the combination of machine and human was later proved to be better than the machine alone.

By continuously incorporating input from human experts, researchers from MIT's Computer Science and Artificial Intelligence Laboratory (CSAIL) and the machine-learning start-up PatternEx have developed an AI platform that predicts cyber-attacks significantly better than existing systems. They called this platform "AI2," which refers to merging AI with "analyst intuition." In this case, the combined effort from human experts and intelligent machines is estimated to reduce false positives by a factor of 5. "The more attacks the system detects, the more analyst feedback it receives, which, in turn, improves the accuracy of future predictions," CSAIL research scientist Kalyan Veeramachaneni, who developed AI2 with PatternEx, says. "That human-machine interaction creates a beautiful, cascading effect."[70]

Often our goals, ideas and dreams are complex, so much so that any single machine cannot accomplish our goals independently. Though machines can do many tasks far better than humans, they do need the help of humans in executing the complex ideas and attaining specific outcomes.

The more complex and sophisticated our dreams are, more human intervention will be required to achieve them.

While there are massive job losses due to automation, there is an equally promising opportunity in racing *with* machines. We all know the power of teamwork. Teamwork often provides better outcomes than any individual contribution can, because the team has a combination of skills that no single individual can possibly have.

As humans talk to each other and understand each other's capabilities, expectations and challenges, they can complement each other seamlessly and produce the required effort collectively to accomplish complex tasks.

During the past three years, I have personally seen thousands of people facing the competition from automation. They find their skills are of no value in the industry and some of them lose their jobs, too.

In one of the projects I managed, we automated the process of analyzing aircraft engine log data using the Big Data technologies. Aircraft engines are equipped with hundreds of sensors that generate tons of data. This data is analyzed continuously to monitor the health of each engine and forecast its health for the next flight and the possibility for any potential issues.

Before this project, a qualified engineer with an average experience of 5 years used to take 32 hours of time to process data from one aircraft engine. The pilot solution we built completely automated this process and finished the job in less than 3 minutes, i.e. over 600 times faster than a human can do. Not just that, while human engineers process data for each engine separately, our analytical model can process data from up to 200 engines simultaneously and still finish the entire job in 3 minutes.

This project initially raised concerns among engineers that their jobs are at stake. However, we insisted on promoting this solution and selling it to our customers. If we didn't do this, our competitors will do it eventually, and all our engineers will lose their jobs. Instead, we did this and encouraged our engineers to apply their skills to go beyond what was traditionally done, such as predicting the upcoming failures and identifying the individual components that need to repaired or replaced.

It helped our engineers not just save their jobs, but to find their calling to do more and thrive in an industry swept by automation.

The only segment of "jobs" that has shown significant growth since 1983 was "Non-Routine Cognitive Jobs." In other words, solving problems with one's creative mind. This is exactly what we need to do in the second machine age. It is just that some of our team members are the machines.

Look for jobs that require creativity, empathy and insight, jobs that need heuristic approach to solve problems. When your job needs heuristic approach, you often don't know exactly what problem you'll be tackling on any given day, or perhaps the parameters for success are constantly changing. For many people, a job or career won't be entirely algorithmic or heuristic. Instead, jobs fall on more of a spectrum with algorithmic tasks at one end and heuristic at the other. The key to win the race against machines is by carefully choosing your skills that can take you from algorithmic work to heuristic work.

In the 21st century workplace, you will be working with a variety of colleagues. Some of your colleagues may not be humans, and may not even look like robots. They can be in the form of a computer or invisible programs in the cloud. Our success depends on how comfortable and efficient we are in working with those intelligent machines. Futurist Kevin Kelly says, "You will be paid in the future based on how well you work with robots."[71]

The idea that all visible and invisible intelligence contributes toward accomplishing tasks at the workplace is the key differentiator for your success. With this understanding, you can see what capabilities are out there, who can do what and, most importantly, what can be achieved through the combination of visible and invisible intelligence.

Understanding the capabilities of machines, identifying the gaps, and complementing them with human intelligence is going to be critical for professional growth in the 21st century.

This is applicable for all industries and all the professional roles across the world. Applying technology to solve problems and create value to society is the sweet spot of dream jobs. Every disruptive technology comes with this golden opportunity.

The Entrepreneurial Mindset

So how can I race with machines? I do not even know how machines work.

Think of machines as your fellow employees; they are better and smarter than you, but never expect more salary or rest than you do. What do you do in such a situation?

You don't want to be an under-performing employee, do you? Then it's time for you to stop being an employee altogether.

Think of your employer instead. It can be your company CEO, other founders, or whoever takes the responsibility of steering your company business to success. What do they do in this situation?

In fact, they feel happy for this situation. They fire you and replace you with a machine that can do your job better. It's a promising future for them. They come up with plans to use these smarter machines for their entrepreneurial activities.

You will know how to race with machines if you can become an entrepreneur or behave like one in your own organization. Not everyone can become an entrepreneur. The good news is that you don't need to become an entrepreneur in order to survive in this economy, but you must have an "entrepreneurial mindset." With an entrepreneurial mindset, you complement the intelligent machines and help them work for your company, for your fellow employees, and for the society.

An entrepreneurial mindset is the single most sought-after skill in the 21st century.

The entrepreneurial mindset (in its many forms) is the definitive road-map for humans to win out over machines today. It's the competitive advantage over machines and a clear differentiator at the workplace.

Computers are not asking interesting new questions. That ability still seems to be uniquely human and is highly valuable in the second machine age. As an entrepreneur, your job is to ask the right questions and work with your team to figure out the answers—of course with the help of machines.

An entrepreneurial mindset is an acquired skill. You can learn this by practice. In fact, entrepreneurship is a *life* idea, not a strictly business one. Again, our roots go back to our evolutionary history for this. We are born entrepreneurs. For millennia, we survived on our individual effort, without being affiliated with any organization. To survive, we created plans and tools to secure food, shelter and a safe environment. We are all entrepreneurs—not because we should start companies, but because the will to create is encoded in our DNA, and creation is the essence of entrepreneurship.

So, I need an entrepreneurial mindset to successfully race with machines. That leads me to the next question: What does the entrepreneurial mindset look like and how can I get it?

7 Qualities of Entrepreneurs

In order to create wealth, entrepreneurs consistently demonstrate the following qualities:

1. Entrepreneurs are great adapters.

   They understand that change is inevitable and change is what creates opportunities. They are continuously looking for change and are always ready to adapt to it, because adaptability creates stability. They thrive on uncertainty. They seem to be inherently creative, because they are inherently adaptive. They seem to be positive and optimistic because they are inherently adaptive.

2. Entrepreneurs are continuous learners.

They understand that change creates new rules. In order to play the game effectively, you need to master the new rules, so you never stop learning. They continuously look for opportunities to improve. They invest in *themselves* before investing in any other endeavors. They are hands-on. They become known as experts in their field.

This is the reason that successful entrepreneurs are naturally good at selling, people skills, negotiation skills, communication skills, managing their money, networking, etc. because they consciously focus on the areas that matter and learn them. They are naturally confident because they know they are sufficiently prepared for the situation.

3. Entrepreneurs accept failure as just another learning step.

They see only two outcomes out of every endeavor: success or learning. They are not afraid to take risks, as long as they are calculated risks. They are always open for experimentation to learn new things and, along the way, at times they succeed.

4. Entrepreneurs develop their passion by building expertise.

They *seem* to be passionate about what they do, but the truth is that they build their passion after they build their expertise. They believe that expertise leads to passion, not the other way around. They don't follow passion blindly. They do not wait until they figure out their passion. They understand that passion needs to be developed through hard work, by developing expertise.

5. Entrepreneurs get motivation from their work.

They don't depend on their motivation to move forward. They understand that motivation is the outcome of intermittent successes. They focus on defined outcomes and hard work to realize those outcomes. For them, motivation follows work, not the other way around.

6. Entrepreneurs are always selling.

They acquire the qualities necessary for selling all the time: Tech savvy. Accessible. Resourceful. Balanced. Organized. Persistent. Determined. Independent. Plan everything.

7. Entrepreneurs have functional humility.

They understand that their egos are only useful in moving the idea forward, not for dictating outcomes or wrestling to make results conform to a preconceived notion. They're willing to listen and learn. They are solution-focused, not idea-focused. They are determined about their vision, but are not attached to the individual ideas that could lead to their vision.

Although they generate and promote their own ideas, they think and act collaboratively to realize the outcomes, and are humble enough to change their ideas if needed. Their humility lets them exit from their plans when it no longer makes sense to pursue them.

Practicing the Entrepreneurial Mindset

You may think that the entrepreneurial mindset does not sound familiar to you. Trust me, it is not difficult to master when you understand the extent you need to learn and adopt it.

First of all, you don't need to be an innovator to win against machines. You don't need to invent new products or services to avoid losing your job to machines. You don't need to come up with new ideas all the time to create the additional revenue opportunities. You don't need to invent new problems that can be solved with new technologies.

It is often the existing problems— the day-to-day challenges and well-known issues at the workplace—that you can try to solve, either totally or partially, with the power of disruptive technologies. We often do things in the same way because of our access to knowledge and systems that achieve a certain level of productivity. It's the mindset to constantly explore better ideas for solving existing problems that gives you the opportunities to identify simple ways to create value.

Irrespective of your past experience, you can find your dream job in emerging technologies when you approach the market with the entrepreneur's mindset. Make up your mind to be ready to come up with promising ideas and solutions that will solve existing problems through the new capabilities offered by these technologies.

Today, no organization uses postal mail service for daily communication needs among their employees because we have email, the most cost effective and quick solution. Similarly, in next couple of decades, organizations will not need to learn about the problems in their products from their customers, because they can monitor their products directly, using the IoT capabilities.

The new capabilities offer new opportunities to solve problems. Often you don't even need to come up with original ideas. Just look at other industries where a particular disruptive technology is more mature.

It's not always about earning more money for the organization. You need to think in multiple dimensions in order to create value. You can focus on reducing cost, improving productivity, security of physical and digital assets, safety of employees and even having more fun at the workplace. All of those contribute to creating value and make you a valuable and indispensable player.

Some technologies are useful in creating a safer work environment, some may be good for increasing productivity, and some other technologies may be good for enhancing customer satisfaction. Someone has to identify these possibilities and come up with ways to realize them in the workplace. Machines cannot do this, at least until the end of our generation. Hence, there is an opportunity for you to win the race with machines.

Answer the following questions to stimulate your thinking about your own situation:

1. What does it take to win the race with machines?
2. What skills do you need to solve problems at your work place?
3. How to you develop an entrepreneurial mindset?

Chapter 10. The Sexiest Jobs of the 21st Century

"Many of these theories have been killed off only when some decisive experiment exposed their incorrectness... Thus the yeoman work in any science...is done by the experimentalist, who must keep the theoreticians honest."
— Michio Kaku, theoretical physicist

The Big 3 Technologies are in fact the net job destroyers. However, while their upheaval in each and every industry eliminates millions of jobs, they also create sweet spots for dream jobs for those who bring the right skills at the right time.

You see a plethora of ideas mushrooming from so-called career experts on what skills, technologies, courses, certifications, etc. you need to master in order to grab these job opportunities. Whether or not you succeed in following those ideas depends on your ability to try multiple options and find your way through this ambiguity. However, there are certain fundamental skills you need to master in order to thrive in the second machine age.

Authors Erik Brynjolfsson and Andrew Mcafee explain these skills in their book, *The Second Machine Age*. According to them, you need: 1) Large scale pattern recognition; 2) Ideation; and 3) Complex Communication. These are cognitive areas where people still seem to have an advantage over intelligent machines.[72]

But if you look these skills closely, you find that these are the very skills every entrepreneur uses to solve problems and create wealth. They help you create value and thrive in ambiguity. As I mentioned in the previous chapter, if you can acquire an entrepreneur's mindset, you will develop these skills automatically and will be able thrive in the second machine age.

Ideation is by far the most desired skill of any entrepreneur. S/he develops ideas to solve known and unknown problems. S/he is good at recognizing patterns from diverse aspects of life— from personal experience, what s/he learned in school, his/her environment and the data s/he looks at—and uses those patterns to come up with innovative ways to solve problems. S/he is also extremely good at working with others and using their help to solve those problems. Again, developing an entrepreneurial mindset can help you gain all of these skills automatically.

In general, applying an entrepreneur's mindset works to secure a dream job in disruptive technologies. However, understanding the role of the technology in business helps you shorten your journey to your dream job.

Each of the three disruptive technologies (IoT, AI and 3D printing) take different approaches to get into them. Understanding their nature and what it takes to get dream jobs is important if you want to get into any of them. While the fundamental skills do not vary, it's often how you apply them in your situation that is the key. Let us see how to apply the entrepreneur mindset to find dream jobs in The Big 3 Technologies:

The Sexiest Jobs in Big Data and Artificial Intelligence

AI is predominantly driven by data and the ability to extract insights from data and to apply those insights to solve the real-life problems. As the amount of data is growing across the world at exponential rates, using AI on the data to solve problems is a growing business need today.

In one of its articles in 2012, Harvard business review stated that the data scientist is the sexiest job of the 21st century.[73] However, using data, a data scientist alone can't solve most of today's problems. A working AI solution needs a lot more than a data scientist, and you can play an important role here from a domain, experience, and business opportunity point of view.

According to quantitative analysis firm Quid, AI has attracted more than $17 billion in investments since 2009. In 2013 alone, more than $2 billion was invested in 322 companies with AI-like technology[74]. Yahoo, Intel, Dropbox, LinkedIn, Pinterest, and Twitter have all purchased AI companies since 2013.

How to identify job opportunities in AI

Large-scale pattern recognition is one of the key hallmarks of today's Big Data-processing technologies. Artificial intelligence can answer questions that humans may not be able to answer. However, AI and other Big Data technologies have some limitations that are opening up enviable opportunities for humans. Their world is limited to the availability of data. They can't do much when there is little data or poor data.

We humans have evolved to understand obscure concepts, summarize vague situations and internalize the essence of complex ideas. We can easily spot relevant concepts, identify patterns and derive meaningful inferences, irrespective of the availability of data.

Though we say that we have Big Data already, in the coming decades, we will see even bigger data, on a scale beyond our imagination. This is just the beginning. Most of our daily transactions are being digitized, but even today a majority of our work life and an even greater part of our personal life is oblivious to the intelligent machines.

In order to identify the opportunities for AI-driven solutions in your work, focus on bridging the gap between the available data and the missing data. You need to identify areas in your work that can be moved into the realm of AI.

Computers are increasingly getting better at processing huge amounts of data in real time. AI is taking over many of the cognitive tasks that the human mind does effortlessly, such as reasoning, planning, learning, natural language processing, perception, and the ability to move and manipulate objects. Over millions of years, humans have acquired and continuously improved these skills, but we are biologically wired with innate limitations on the amount of data we can handle and the speed at which we can process it. Machines are transcending these limitations and opening up a new world for us.

Understanding human cognitive limitations helps you come up with compelling ideas on what AI can do for your business. As the majority of the work in organizations is already automated, the problems we face at our workplace become increasingly complex.

We need to handle processes that we could not otherwise handle without those machines. Any malfunction in those machines may create a disruption in daily business that a human possibly cannot handle. You need higher intelligence to fix problems created by machines. This is another area where humans find opportunities for building new automation systems.

Ask yourself these questions:

1. What are the areas in your daily job that you find increasingly difficult to do, perhaps because of increasing complexity?

2. What are the tasks that a super-intelligent person (imagine that there is such a thing) can do better than you can?

When you ask yourself these questions, don't become frightened that you may lose your job. You *will* eventually lose your current job, even if you do not bring this idea forward.

All you have is the time between now and when somebody else brings this idea forward and it is implemented. Why don't you take the lead and introduce better way of doing things at your workplace? That's the role left for humans in the workplace of tomorrow. In the coming decades, we are going to see this more and more, in every aspect of our working lives.

Think of your utopian workplace with the following preconditions:

1. Ubiquity of data: Imagine that everything is datafied.
2. Abundance of computing power
3. Machine intelligence mimicking the human mind and exceeding it

With these preconditions, ask yourself:

1. With these capabilities in place, how do you see your business running on a day-to-day basis?
2. What processes can you automate with AI?
3. Where do you eliminate humans altogether?
4. What else you can do with these capabilities to improve your business?

You get it, right?

Once you build an idea for introducing AI at your workplace, communicating your idea is also quite challenging because it still looks like science fiction at the moment.

Complex communication is less about mastering the art of communication and more about understanding what drives people in your organization and crafting your message accordingly.

You may want to prepare a plan to convince your boss, because you know him/her better. However, it is essential to validate your ideas against the organizational drivers first. Every organization is driven by key metrics such as revenue, profitability, customer and employee satisfaction, etc. Have a clear plan for how your solution is going to influence some of these key metrics that your organization deems important. Having a clear, measurable and demonstrable plan is essential, before you even attempt to disclose your idea to your key stakeholders.

You may want to validate your ideas with your peers before you take them to the decision makers, because if the latter see a lack of clarity in your plan, they may not give you a second chance.

If you look at it carefully, the complex communication has two parts to it. First is the idea itself. The completeness of your idea defines whether you are ready or not. You need to spend majority of your time on validating your idea. The rest goes to the second part of communication, which is the physical articulation of the idea and convincing others of its value.

Identifying the organizational metrics and mapping them with your respective stakeholders can give you a fair idea of who is interested in what. The next step is to find how your solution can influence each of those metrics. Emphasize the impact of those metrics to the people who care about them the most. If you can come up with an example or an apt story, that would be great.

Your communication abilities may play some role here, but not significantly if you are thorough with your first step, which is the completeness of the idea itself.

Although the potential to use AI at workplace is huge, I recommend that you choose only the proven solutions in your industry as well as other industries. Industrialization of AI has a long way to go. When you pick up something already in use somewhere, it becomes easier to convince your stakeholders, unless you are a technical architect who can demonstrate the feasibility.

You can refer to the examples of AI that are already working, such as Google search, Amazon product recommendations, Facebook friend suggestions, etc., but you cannot depend on them only. These are futuristic technologies, built by some of the best minds on the planet today. Considering the limited budget and timelines your business has, what can you offer to your business? Identify what falls into that bucket; you would rather make it easy to get it accepted by others.

The Sexiest Jobs in IoT

Entrepreneurs see IoT as a once-in-a-lifetime opportunity to make their millions. However, they do not find it easy to realize that dream, even though the technology is promising. They know that it is possible to monitor anything and connect with other things that make sense, so they are trying to create functional utility from these capabilities.

In case you are into technical development, here are some of the most demanding technical skills in IoT today:[75]

1. Circuit Design: Smart devices are built with Printed Circuit Boards (PCBs) that need to be designed for a specific purpose.

2. Microcontroller Programming: Every connected device has a micro-controller that needs to be programmed for its intended purpose.

3. AutoCAD: A mushrooming number of devices need new design standards and personalization.
4. Security Infrastructure: Device, network and data security
5. Node.js: An open-source language used to manage connected devices

These technical jobs constitute less than 20% of the overall IoT ecosystem. The remaining jobs are for those who are willing to learn and aspire to take them. I focus more on those jobs.

The most challenging part in this is finding the applicability, usability of monitoring, and control by smart things. You need a sound domain understanding to assess the usability and its economic impact in an overall business.

IoT has barely touched the monitoring job in most of the industries. Cross-communication among multiple things and controlling is hardly realized.

Of course, in order to achieve this level of sophistication (at the moment), there are technological limitations, too. However, the key challenge remains in the identification of the case for use itself and this is exactly where you can find the coveted job opportunities. If you are already working in an industry, you are the best person to assess what additional data and remote monitoring would add value to your business.

IoT is blurring the difference between physical and digital systems. Irrespective of their size, most *physical* devices, tools and utilities will also have their *digital* interface, to connect with humans as well as with other connected things.

So what is our role in bringing in this world of tomorrow?

Surprisingly, it is not necessarily the technical know-how that is most needed. Technically, everything and anything can be datafied, monitored, controlled and connected with other things today.

The real challenge lies in identifying what connection makes sense, what interoperability creates value, and which connections make economic sense. This is something machines can't do, at least for now.

We already see products on the market that connect and monitor all sorts of things, such as pets and plants. Some of the products may sound silly and may not even be successful. This is possibly because the entrepreneur who brought such products into the market did not understand the domain. That's the gap you may fill in.

In your work experience, you are the best person to identify things that make better sense for connecting and monitoring. This is where entrepreneurs and existing businesses need your help. You already know the challenges in your current job and in your current business.

Your experience, coupled with knowledge of the IoT technology capabilities, is the key to your success. Imagine your industry and especially your role in a utopian IoT world.

Think of your utopian workplace with the following preconditions:

1. Everything that you use at your workplace and beyond is connected with every other thing.
2. It is possible to know every behavior of those things from the past and in real time.
3. It is even possible to predict common behaviors that will be exhibited by those things in the immediate future.

With these preconditions, ask yourself:

1. With these capabilities in place, how do you see your business running on a day-to-day basis?
2. In this situation/environment, how do solve your current challenges at your workplace?
3. Where do you eliminate humans altogether?
4. What else can you do with these capabilities to improve your business?

These questions can help you identify opportunities with IoT. Jot down your ideas and start validating them one at a time. This utopia is being uncovered slowly, thanks to these disruptive technologies, but you can be the pioneer for this journey.

You can develop valuable ideas with IoT by understanding the technology's capabilities and the benefits derived from overlapping it with other disruptive technologies, such as AI and robotics. The combination of 3D printing and IoT will be a huge business opportunity in the near future, possibly post-2020.

To generate more ideas, I talk to business owners and technology architects. I understand the current business challenges and their utopian ideas from business owners/heads and go back to consult either bestselling books or competent technology architects who can give me ideas on how to solve those hypothetical problems.

Something you need to note here is the need for describing the business problem so that a technical architect can understand it. If you ask any technical-possibility-related question, architects can answer it almost immediately.

You need to translate the business problems into individual technology capabilities, get them validated from architects, and then integrate them back into a feasible solution.

Another way to come up with innovative ideas is by following other industries. Often the innovation can be cross-pollinated to bring forth compelling ideas. Who knows? Sometimes the applicability of an existing solution can be more appreciated in your business, even if it was already tried and tested in some other industry but was not a great success there.

Many start-ups have learned their lessons the hard way by developing so-called smart things, such as smart electric switches, espresso machines, propane tanks, etc. However, these applications (a.k.a. failure stories) gave stunning ideas to others who could build a successful start-up elsewhere.[76]

The Sexiest Jobs in 3D Printing

Most of the revolutionary technologies such as Big Data and IoT had to grow immensely in the virtual world before impacting the physical world. Their effect on the physical world is marginal compared to their growth and maturity in virtual world.

Consider 3D printing in that sense. It is the direct translation of a virtual world into our physical reality. It's the direct channel from our imagination to physical reality. Its impact is more direct and profound. 3D printing impacts not just the manufacturing industry alone, but almost all the other industries, as well.

Why the sexiest jobs are in 3D printing

After AI, I think 3D printing is the second-greatest job destroyer. However, its massive disruption is leading to a huge imbalance in demand/supply equation of certain skills. That's where you can find some of the golden career opportunities.

Before 1440 (when Johannes Gutenberg invented the printing press), people used to copy books by hand, which would often take more than a year for each book. As this was a slow and painstaking process that often incurred mistakes, many people used to be employed for this purpose. In spite of this, very few books were published, and they were available primarily to churches and scholars. By the turn of that century, printing shops appeared in every major city across Europe, and there were more than 6 million copies of books in circulation.[77]

During this period, manual book copiers suddenly became irrelevant in their society and lost their jobs. Apart from them, highly regarded teachers lost their unique authority on their subject, because gifted students no longer needed to sit at the feet of their masters in order to learn new skills. At the same time, there was a new breed of entrepreneurs that started flourishing through printing books and newspapers.

This situation was rather predictable, but then something more profound and unexpected happened. The Catholic Church, which had been the custodian of ideas and wisdom for more than a millennium, quickly lost control of the spread of ideas, as more and more books of a secular nature were published.

Scientists working across Europe got access to accurate (not miscopied by humans) information from the work done by other scientists. In the next two centuries, the availability of this transparent and unfettered knowledge led to multiple inventions that ultimately led to the industrial revolution.

While the printing press, photocopier and Internet helped us spread ideas rapidly, 3D printing lets our ideas go from the second dimension to the third. Every additional capability in this process made ideas less protected in our society.

With 3D printing accessible to everyone, it becomes even harder to keep ideas and things from being copied. Those exclusive physical objects, which were once perceived to be private and elite, can now be mimicked, reused and exploited.

Once again, to get entrepreneurial ideas, imagine your industry (and especially your role) in a utopian 3D-printing world.

Think of your utopian workplace with the following preconditions:

1. Everything that you see and use at your workplace and beyond can be manufactured using 3D printing.
2. It is possible to modify the design of those things to any extent and produce just one piece to test your ideas.
3. It is also possible to add/extend the products you use (or think of using) to/with any other thing(s).

With these preconditions, ask yourself:

1. With these capabilities in place, how do you see your business running on a day-to-day basis?
2. In this environment, how do you solve your current challenges at your workplace?
3. If your organization is selling a product, think of ways to produce it using 3D-printing technology. If you think it is not feasible to produce the entire product using 3D printing, can you produce any of its components that way?
4. Where do you eliminate humans altogether?

Mass customization is one of the areas where you can find your dream jobs in 3D printing. Industrialization and mass production taught us how to produce common things that suit many of our customers.

Today, there are hardly any low-value products in the market that are only made for one customer. This trend is going to be reversed. 3D printing allows us to produce just one product, without worrying about the cost.

Most of the products will be eventually transformed into unlimited variations, according to the taste of individual customers. Your dream job lies in making this change possible.

The data scientist is not the only sexy job in the 21st century. In fact, with the pace of change in artificial intelligence, the data scientist job has already lost its sheen because today some of the capabilities of the data scientist have already been automated by AI.

If you have an entrepreneurial mindset, you can find the sexiest jobs in any disruptive technology and in any industry. It is the gateway to create your dream job wherever you like. You don't need to aim for The Big 3 Technologies alone for your dream job. I used them only as examples to find opportunities. In the next Section, I will give you a proven system to find your dream job in any emerging technology that you wanted.

Answer the following questions to stimulate your thinking about your own situation:

1. What are the fundamental skills that are needed to thrive in the second machine age? How do you acquire them?
2. How do you find sexiest jobs in AI?
3. How do you find sexiest jobs in IoT?
4. How do you find sexiest jobs in 3D printing?

Section 3
CRACKING THE CODE OF THE DREAM JOB

Chapter 11. Finding Your Path to Freedom

"Until we see what we are, we cannot take steps to become what we should be." —Charlotte P. Gilman

For some people, changing jobs is like changing cars. For others, it's like changing their spouse. And for yet some others, it's like changing their gender. Some do it at most once or never do it in their lifetime. Some do it quite often.

In any case, transforming their career through job-switching is the journey of a lifetime for anyone. You may find it easy to find another job in your own industry and area of expertise, but when you want to switch your industry or even to a different functional area within your own industry, you need a lot more courage and preparation.

Understand Yourself Better

Though it's not common, many people attempt to make mid-career switches to a totally different industry. It's not often better pay or any other seemingly attractive thing that motivates such a change. Something beyond that comes into play, such as passion or the drive to make a meaningful contribution. Such a strong drive to change your career and life is possible when you understand yourself better. You need to know your strengths and weaknesses, values and priorities.

We all know our interests and even (to some extent) our passions in some ways, but we often don't have enough courage to pursue our passions. We are not sure about our passions, our capabilities, the opportunities we see in the market. Sometimes we are also not sure whether we could become successful by following our passion.

This lack of clarity leaves us living most of our lives in desperation.

Thanks to the pioneering research in human psychology over the last two centuries, today it's not that difficult to understand your natural talents and even your values.

We have some proven systems available today to help us understand ourselves better, to make meaningful choices in life, and be happier. I suggest you read the book *Strengths Finder2.0*[78] and take the online test that comes free with the book.

Strengths Finder2.0 was written by Tom Rath, who spent 13 years in Gallup, the leading research and consulting firm, on employee engagement, strengths and well-being. I took this test and found it very useful for finding my strengths, weaknesses, and (more importantly) what to do with them to attain my desired outcomes in life.

After taking this test, I understood that it is significantly more valuable and fun to leverage my strengths, instead of trying to fix all of my weaknesses. It's the choice you need to make between multiplication of results using your strengths, or incremental improvement by fixing weaknesses that will, at best, become mediocre. Focus on the better use of your best tools instead of wasting your time on constant repairs.

Many of us have a vague idea on our strengths and weaknesses because we keep hearing them from others, when they say that we are good at this and that. Sometimes we are rewarded for our best qualities, and that raises our confidence.

But how often do you work seriously on the skills that others say you are really good at? Scientific assessments (such as *Strength Finder2.0*) not only help you to identify your strengths, but also show you what you need to do to take advantage of those strengths. When such an unbiased scientific body approves your strengths, you start believing in yourself and your confidence improves accordingly.

For example, one of my strengths (per my *Strengths Finder 2.0* assessment) is "responsibility." I feel personally responsible for what I say I will do for others. It's important to me that I have to honor my commitments. Before taking this test, I used to feel bad for many days whenever I broke even a minor commitment to others, such as returning a call, sending a piece of information, etc.

After I knew that responsibility is my strength and inner value, I don't make any commitments if I think I can't honor them, but when I make commitments, I ensure that I honor them all of the time, so the pain of neglecting my responsibility has gone forever. This just eliminates the inner psychological burden. What about using my strength for my growth? Yes, it helped me there, even more. I have better clarity while choosing the opportunities that arise at my workplace. I don't take everything that comes to me. I am open and careful about my priorities, which enables me to save more time and to spend quality time on the things that matter to me.

Knowing yourself strengthens you with regard to the abilities you already possess. Becoming more aware of them leads you to use them for greater success and that, in turn, generates more enthusiasm, creating a positive, upward spiral in which you feel better about yourself and what you do.

Understand What Success Means to You

Let me break down the process of your journey to success.

At a broader level, there are external forces and your response to them. External forces are opportunities—what you might call luck, serendipity, the right time and the right place for you, etc.

On the other hand, how do you structure your response to the external forces so that it contains everything that a human can possibly do? You also need to acknowledge your action and take control if needed.

Everything that affects your reaction to the environment falls into three buckets:

1. Your resources,
2. The processes you follow to reach your goals, and
3. Your priorities.

These are applicable to everyone. Resources are what you already possess: your property, money, education, skills, experience, your network and all the other things that you can possibly use in your efforts to make use of the opportunities that life throws at you. The easy way to identify your resources by attributing a monetary value to them in one way or another.

The processes are HOW you use your resources to seek what you want in your life. These are the ways you choose to move ahead in your day- to-day life. You may be thinking that you respond to opportunities according to your resources. Of course your resources can influence your processes, but they cannot uniquely define them. That's why everyone does not behave exactly the same in a given situation. Unlike your resources, your processes are not visible to others. They are not written anywhere, so it is difficult to keep track of them.

Your processes are more important than your resources in your journey to success. We have seen many stories about "rags to riches," but when it comes our personal situation, it's difficult for us to believe that those stories apply to us.

We often blame our lack of resources for our failures and ignore the fact that our approach (the process) to solving our problems and for grabbing opportunities may be wrong.

The third and the most important among these is your priorities. They define WHAT you choose to pursue in your life. Your priorities are shaped by your aspirations, interests and values. They are more important than both your resources and processes combined, because ultimately they define your happiness.

If you are trying to build more resources for yourself while ignoring your priorities, you are actually creating conflict in yourself. *Resources are meaningful only when they are aligned with your priorities.* Somebody is ready to pay millions of dollars for a piece of art that, for billions of other people is only worth a penny.

Our inner voice tells us what is important for us, but we often ignore it because our family, friends and sometimes our society tells us a different story. We become confused and follow the crowd for the comfort of being accepted and fitting in with those in our close social circles.

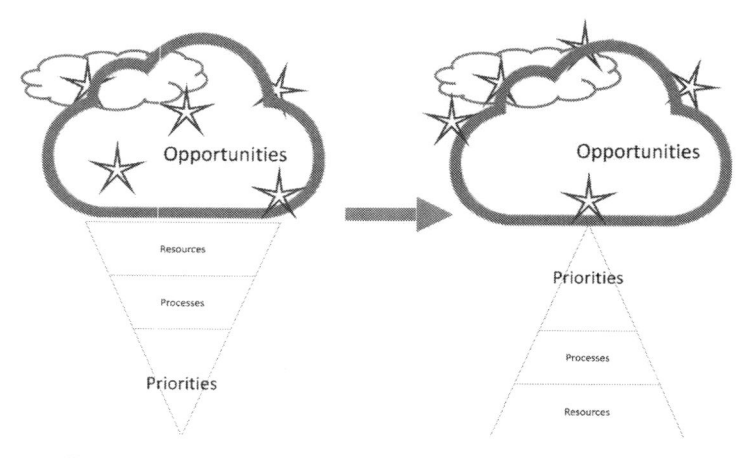

Figure 7. Priorities-driven approach to seek opportunities.

As shown in the figure 7, when people see the cloud of opportunities around them, they try to choose among them based on their available resources. If you believe that your *resources* can get you the opportunity you see (not necessarily the one you need), you often ignore looking for *the right process* to win that opportunity.

Your reliance on your resources makes you believe that you do not need anything else to succeed, in spite of the fact that we often notice that people do succeed in our society, with or without resources.

Not only that, there is an even bigger problem with this approach. When you are not being guided by your priorities, you will be guided by the external forces that may or may not give you the satisfaction that you seek.

When you look at an opportunity that is highly valued by your colleagues or friends, you automatically start giving it more value, irrespective of whether it is valuable for you or not. It is only after you have made your decision and started living your life within that opportunity that you start questioning your judgment because you don't find what you were expecting from it.

On the other hand, when you begin with your priorities as a focus, you can more easily recognize the opportunities that will bring you more happiness. You go the extra mile to find the suitable process to grab that opportunity because you are driven by your inner voice. Some people call this passion. When you are driven by your priorities, you not only use your resources effectively, but you also build the right resources that are needed to succeed.

This approach is much more important today than ever because of the abundance of choices we are exposed to. In today's world, if you do not choose your opportunities wisely, it's easier to become overwhelmed and lose one's way than it is to be focused and attain what one seeks. You need to identify your priorities, processes and resources, and then act accordingly.

What It Takes to Become an Achiever

There is one more important thing you need to work on before you attempt to obtain your dream job: attaining an achiever's mindset.

You will not become an achiever *after* you get what you want. You get what you want because you are *already* an achiever.

What separates achievers from average people, at least externally? We know that high performers have good subject-matter expertise, a skill that is learned and earned over time, but there is something else that is visible more often than this. It is their social skills. Irrespective of the level of subject-matter expertise, people are considered achievers in social situations if they can demonstrate *social skills*, such as confidence, leadership, persuasion, positive optimism and genuine enthusiasm.

Most of us assume that social skills are innate and cannot be learned. In my thinking, understanding that social skills can be learned, practiced, and improved over time is a paradigm shift. It is possible to learn and consistently demonstrate such skills in our workplace and daily life.

It's not rocket science and also not a lengthy subject to master. The polished social skills are reflected in the way people talk, move and express their feelings. While most of the behaviors seem common and indistinguishable, only some of them actually separate achievers from the rest. Let's call them the Competency Triggers. We just need to identify those key behaviors and practice them consistently.

Each one of us is good at something that comes out naturally under certain social situations. Observe yourself. When and in what social situations do you demonstrate high-competence triggers that achievers seemingly demonstrate all of the time?

Let's say you are talking about something while you are surrounded by people who are lower in social status than you are.

How do you feel about it?

You most likely feel confident, enthusiastic and find it easy to convey your point of view to the people around you. You may feel jittery if you are asked to do the exact same thing when your boss is around.

Why do achievers seemingly demonstrate confidence in all situations? Why do you feel less confident when you are surrounded by people whom you perceive are of a higher social status than you? Because you have not learned and automated your high-competence triggers.

Achievers consistently display behaviors that subtly identify them as such. They use certain phrases and practices, often unconsciously.

So, how do I internalize high-competence triggers and habitually demonstrate them?

Simple! Act like an achiever.

It sounds counter-intuitive, but it works beautifully over time.

Yes, from this very moment, you are going to act like an achiever.

To begin your transformative moment now, I suggest you watch the 2012 TED video titled, "Your body language shapes who you are," by Amy Cuddy. (http://www.ted.com/talks/amy_cuddy_your_body_language_shapes_who_you_are) It is one of the most popular talks of all time as of the writing of this book.[79]

I think it would be a "magic bullet" for you to start believing that you can "fake" and actually "become" what you want to become. Amy's findings are the culmination of multiple research studies in this field over the last 100 years.

People have talked about positive thinking before Napoleon Hill published his book "Think and Grow Rich" in 1937. Many people have shown the benefits of positive thinking on their mind and overall well-being. However, applying this principle to a specific outcome, observing yourself, testing to discover which approach works for you, and then adopting it is the key for reaping the true benefit of this idea.

When I experimented with adopting competence triggers, I found that it was taking a long time for me to identify any noticeable result. I have seen people become demotivated and give up.

I tested different approaches to accelerate this process. One of the key things that worked for me is observing myself in social situations and assessing myself. I recorded a video of myself while speaking in front of my laptop webcam. I chose a topic of my interest and spoke for 5 minutes. That video revealed so much about my body language, such as I was not smiling enough, how many times I used non-words, how absurd my pauses were, etc. Later on, I started analyzing my public-speaking videos. Had I not done this, I would have taken a long time to identify my mistakes or I might not have found them at all.

Observing yourself and being brutally honest with yourself helps you to internalize an achiever's mindset.

While I knew about the changes in my thinking, I remember my friends and colleagues telling me about the change in my mindset when I was struggling with my job. At that time, everybody around me knew that I shouldn't be working in that role, and should be looking for a better one. However, they could see that I was giving my best, so I remained stuck until I found a way to internalize an achiever's mindset.

I remember that it all happened in a very short period of time, a few months or so. I still remember the day when the promotions were announced in my previous company and I did not get one for the umpteenth time. After I saw that happen, I applied for leave for a week and came home. I told my wife that I was not afraid; rather I was happy that the time had come for me to change—to change right then. I spent that week searching for my dream job and luckily managed to secure one interview that changed my career forever.

Before you can achieve anything externally, you need to first become an achiever internally. Develop and adopt the mindset of an achiever.

Answer the following questions to stimulate your thinking about your own situation:

1. Do you know what your strengths are? If not, go figure that out first. Then build your action plan, based on your strengths, for the outcomes you want in your life.
2. What's your approach to find the best job opportunities in the market? Start making decisions based on your priorities.
3. Do you have an achiever's mindset? It's something you can learn and build within yourself. Start today, if you are not already working on this.

Chapter 12. Dream Job Principles for the 21st Century

"Learn the rules like a pro, so you can break them like an artist." — Pablo Picasso

"You have to learn the rules of the game, and then you have to play better than anyone else." — Albert Einstein

It's not only the businesses themselves; when it comes to change, the job market is also drastically affected by the shift to disruptive technologies. The pace of change in technology and the way people do business today has made most of the traditional ways for getting a job irrelevant.

Before starting your endeavor toward getting a dream job, it is essential for you to understand the on-the-ground realities. I list 10 of the new realities of today's job market here:

1. Resumes are dead.

Your resume is what *you* say about yourself. It has been valuable in the past because employers did not have other means of knowing about you, but that's not true anymore.

You are letting the world know much more about yourself than you think. What you consciously reveal about yourself is just a tiny part of what you are actually revealing about yourself to the world. Everything that we do online, either consciously or unconsciously, gets recorded.

If you do a transaction on an e-commerce site, the site not only records all the products you browsed, but also the way you browsed, and how much time you spent on each part of the screen. This has become a common practice for all of the major websites.

The data collected about human behavior is becoming increasingly valuable to business, so whoever collects this data has an opportunity to sell it to others. That's how your personal data is shared across multiple platforms and you become their commodity.

Employers are increasingly depending on sources *other than* your resume to understand your fitness for their job requirement. Resumes are dead. It's time to monitor your online profile and to manage it actively.

2. A job portal is the last choice for an employer.

When employers come up with a need for more people or new positions, they first try to fill them up from within their existing employees because they can cut recruiting and initial training costs and fill the positions as soon as possible. They decide to look outside their organization only when they can't find anyone suitable within their organization. But even when they have to look outside, there is a long way to go before employers try out a job portal.

Outside of the organization, the first choice usually goes to the people whom they personally know and whom they perceive of as being good at doing their job. If they can't think of anyone, then they look for strong referrals from their network. When that also does not work, they finally resort to job portals, which are usually the last attempt in any recruiting process.

Duncan Mathison, the co-author of the 2009 book, *Unlock the Hidden Job Market,* says around 50% of positions are usually filled on an informal basis, i.e. either without advertising or only advertising after someone has already been identified internally for the position.[80]

Some of the leading influencers on the job market say that the hidden job market is almost 80%, so what you see on the job portals is just the tip of the iceberg.

3. Networking is the shortest path to the dream job.

There are so many qualified people desperately looking for a job today. Having the right qualifications is just a necessary condition, but you need something more important than that—the right network. In this economy, building the right network is the shortest path to your dream job.

We intuitively establish trust in people and things we see. The more often we see them, the stronger our trust becomes.

Let's say that when you are jogging in a park, you see someone you have never met. Your mind creates an impression of that person without you even being aware of it. When you both see each other again on the following day, or even a few weeks later, you most probably smile at each other this time. You start developing trust in the other person, assuring yourself that the other person is safe to talk to and hang around with.

We have developed this unconscious ability to "read" people and the things we see around ourselves over millions of years, beginning in the wild forests, which were unimaginably dangerous places in which to survive.

It is the same with other things in our life, as well. Imagine you hear news from two different sources on a recent earthquake in a remote location. One is BBC and the other is a local news agency, say XYZ. Which do you trust? You don't want to quote some unrecognized source, especially when you report to others. XYZ news agency could have been the local authority which had better access to the information, but you don't care. You want to refer to the news agency in which you have built your trust.

Now imagine that you are interviewing a bunch of people and you have personally known one person among them. You have met that person, have a good understanding of his/her abilities, and you think that person's abilities match the role you are interviewing for.

It's possible that you hear better answers to your questions from the other people you interviewed that day. However, it's difficult to convince yourself to trust what you hear for the first time from an unknown person than it is to trust hearing the same voice and possibly familiar answers from someone you already know.

You may ask, "But how can I know who is going to interview me?" That seems to be difficult, but it's not impossible. If you have to make an investment for finding your dream job, it is best made in building your network. The payoff from this work is definite and more valuable than searching for 100 other jobs online and patiently preparing customized resumes for each of them.

What if you were previously not able to reach out to anyone from the interview panel? Well, fortunately, it's not a show-stopper. The next best alternative is getting in touch with someone who can influence your interviewer.

I discussed the power of suggestions and recommendations earlier. Social commerce is thriving today because of this. When we do not have any information, we trust our friends to make our decisions. It works equally well in job markets. Try to reach someone who can influence the hiring manager, when you cannot not reach the hiring manager directly.

4. Applying for too many jobs does not increase the possibility of getting hired.

You do want to cast a wider net when it comes to jobs. You don't want to miss out on any opportunities, so you want to be open to anything that seems interesting. But job hunting is totally different from fishing. You don't need many. You just need *one* that is perfect for you.

So you don't need a wider net, but the one that is custom made to catch just one fish. You need to do deeper work on one potential opportunity, rather than shallow work on the entire job market.

5. Qualifications are blurred.

Chris Anderson's "long tail effect" is visible in every industry today. New players are billowing forth, offering innovative products and services in niche markets. These new age employers are looking for skills beyond those that you traditionally list in your resume. No single academic degree, certification, or particular project experience would suffice for them.

You need to reinvent yourself, to make yourself relevant for this industry by equipping yourself beyond traditional qualifications. You need to learn a lot more than what you have learned in school. You need wider exposure to industry challenges than what you have learned in all of your previous jobs. The fast-changing industries and technologies demand that we keep up with them continuously.

6. The common roles are blurred.

In the sequence of filling up positions in any company, the common roles (such as software engineer, HR executive or marketing executive) get filled up first. It's often difficult to find openings for these basic roles because they get filled up, either internally or directly from the campus.

Any roles beyond these starting careers are becoming increasingly difficult to define because of the nature of the changing business environment. It's often easy to find job openings in the market for senior roles, but you may find it difficult to appear qualified for them because they demand so much that you end up lacking one or another of the "must have" requirements.

There are two ways to address this situation. Obviously the first is to develop yourself into a well-rounded personality with minimum exposure to the common roles in your prospective company, and then to focus on a deep expertise in the particular position you are looking for.

The second (and more interesting) option is to ignore the job description, because it is simply a utopian wish from a prospective employer. You don't need to take it for granted as a given and then decide not to apply for it because you don't seem to fit the description. Many times, employers do not get what they look for. They end up choosing the best among the available. If you think you are right for that job, go for it and try to prove how you can do that and why you are the right fit for it.

7. Not all positions are urgent. Perseverance pays.

Employers do not usually start hunting for people as soon as they identify a need. In general, open positions are identified in long-term planning, so the employer feels no urgency to fill them immediately.

On the other hand, the need for a specific position may surface as the business grows beyond expectations. In both the cases, employers tend to continue with the status quo until it really starts to impact their business.

This is why, even though the recruitment process is initiated and people are being evaluated for an open position, employers keep on looking for the best candidates until the position becomes an urgent necessity.

When you attend an interview, you can't wait for the recruiter's response. You expect the response next day. But your perception of "yesterday" is a split second for employers. They may need a longer time to respond to you—a few weeks or even months.

If you didn't get a response in a week or two, you may think you were not selected, but you need to be persistent. You can use this time to build your network. In fact, the longer an employer waits to convey the decision, the greater the opportunity you have to influence them.

8. Not all interviewers are equally important.

When you are called for 5, 6 or even more rounds of interviews, you may think every round is an elimination round. It need not be. There are some people in an organization who need to be involved in the recruitment process just as a formality.

Usually, there is only one person responsible for making the final decision on whether to hire you or not. It's your hiring manager or your future boss, if s/he is senior enough to hire you. But s/he needs to (or may want to) get agreement from various other people so that s/he can be held less accountable, just in case you end up being a misfit later on.

How do you know who is the real decision maker and who is not? Check out their role and relationship to the department you are being interviewed for. If you miss this before the interview, check for other clues during the interview.

The non-critical interviewers may find themselves having no time for your interview. They also ask questions in no particular sequence, or even without any specific intention. Their feedback is still important for your success. However, you need a different type of preparation to clear such interviews.

You need to know the professional background of interviewer and talk her language. If you could not know about her before entering into your interview room, it's ok to ask her name and her key responsibilities in business. All you need to do is make sure that you make sense to her if she needs you for anything in future.

9. Experience outside of your day job is fine, too.

Don't wait until you get an opportunity to work on your dream technology area. You may not ever get it. Today, knowledge and personal experience in the area is valued, and not necessarily from experience in a full-time job.

If you are a technology expert, consider the following options to gain experience in a new technology:

1. Take up a side project. Start working on it right away in your free time. Once you learn the technology, look for challenges in online forums such as TopCoder, GitHub, Kaggle, etc. Your value in the market will be increased more than you think, if you can manage to contribute to these forums. Even if you are lucky enough to get full-time work experience in any technology, most probably you will end up working on a small subset of the growing technology area. In order to claim mastery over the subject and qualify yourself in the job market, it is essential that you learn outside of your job experience and take on projects that can prove your overall skills.

2. Volunteer within your organization. If your organization is already working on your area of interest, request to work for the respective department voluntarily. It's not illegal. If you are willing to work over and above your responsibilities, you are treated as a motivated employee.

3. Work for free. Not everyone may find it feasible to leave their current job and work for some other company for free, but it is definitely worth considering if you can afford it. You have the freedom to choose some of the best available technology problems/people/organizations to work for. Your chances of getting a dream job become multiplied many times over when you get the right experience from the right people in the industry.

If you are not into technology, but you are looking for a job on the business side of any exponential technology, consider the following options:

1. Write. Develop a broad understanding of the technology, primarily from the point of view of applications and creating business value. Start writing on this topic, either on your own blog or for public online forums. The ability to express ideas is one of the key skills in demand today. Doing it for a growing technology area gives you quicker visibility in the market. Of course, you need to learn a lot before you can start writing about it, but believe me, it's not difficult. I have done this in multiple technologies by now. The easiest way to start this journey is by reading the bestselling books on the subject. Go to amazon.com and pick up the top 10 books on the subject. Buy and read them. You will become more knowledgeable than 99% of the people in that industry after that.

2. Volunteer within your organization. Once you demonstrate your knowledge through writing, you can offer your voluntary work in areas such as pre-sales, business development, marketing, alliances, etc. if your organization is already in business in the particular technology space.

3. Work for free. This is another rewarding option, if you can afford it.

If you are ambitious, speaking about your dream technology is another promising way to find great opportunities in the industry. Again, it's not difficult. You need to learn the technology and possibly write a few articles before you can convince someone to use you for speaking about it to others.

The easiest way to start this journey is by reaching out to your university and offering them a guest lecture. Universities usually welcome their alumni for speaking, either on their industry experience or on emerging technologies. Once you manage to speak at your university, you can use *that* experience to find opportunities to speak at business conferences and other professional events. Start working on this. You will find it much easier than you think, and it's a great way to increase your exposure in the field.

10. Education outside of college is essential.

Education outside of college is not optional; it's essential today. It is becoming almost impossible for traditional educational institutions to keep pace with the emerging technologies and be relevant in the industry.

You don't need years of master's degree work, but a short and specific course, after which you can start working right away. And your learning does not stop there. As you take up new challenges in these rapidly changing industries, you need to learn continuously, to keep yourself relevant.

Massive Open Online Courses (MOOCs) are the future of education. You don't need to spend tons of money on college degrees anymore. Just choose the one you need right now, and finish that in the next 3 months or so. You are good to go for now, but keep watching for the next valuable skill. Most of these courses are for free and at the most, some cost a few hundred dollars.

Courses taken from leading MOOC providers such as Coursera, edX, Udacity, etc. are equally valued (if not more) in the job market, just like those traditional college degrees.

If you are serious about your job prospects, take learning seriously. Education is already democratized. You can get some of the best education in the world for almost free. Make use of it.

These 10 ideas are the new rules of today's job market. They help you get the right mindset to approach that job market successfully. Ignore them at your risk.

In the next chapter, I will present the step by step method I followed to find my dream job. I have helped hundreds of my students get their dream jobs by using this same method.

Answer the following questions to stimulate your thinking about your own situation:

1. What are the new rules of the job market?
2. Which of these rules sound contrary to your existing beliefs, or at least, to what you were doing before?
3. How do you need to modify your approach to follow the new rules?

Chapter 13. The Definitive Roadmap to Your Dream Job

"People would do better, if they know better." — Jim Rohn

"Whenever you find yourself on the side of the majority, it is time to pause and reflect." — Mark Twain

For the major part of my career, the only way I knew to get a job was to send out my resume and wait for a reply. I never did anything beyond sending my resume and praying for success. At times, I used to slightly modify my resume by adding some keywords that were asked for in the job description and then send it across. That's all I did, until I found a different way that worked like a magic.

My prolonged struggle with a corporate IT job, searching for meaning, job satisfaction and a respectable position based on my experience and skills, left me feeling desolate. I thought that the more time I spent in that job, the less skilled I became.

We used to say to our colleagues that we got systematically de-skilled in our jobs, so that we couldn't either find a better job outside or ask for a raise in that company. The daily dose of the degeneration of my soul started being reflected in other areas of my life. It was from this state that I found a path to break out of that cycle.

There were always one or two key motives that used to drive my job search. It was either higher salary or a better role, or both. My job hunting was a painful experience. The results from multiple job interviews were just ordinary, similar to what all my other average friends used to get. I was fed up with this and wanted to try something else.

Getting a job is a difficult process, so we often try to delegate that responsibility to recruiters and friends. It's easy to send out a resume online or to a friend who we expect would forward it to the right people and bring us good fortune.

Most of us think that others need to help us get our job. We think our responsibility is just to send out a resume. We even feel productive when we apply for multiple jobs in a day, but end up feeling disappointed when we see the poor response we get with that approach.

In hindsight, I see that I was so lucky to somehow get the inspiration, explore the unexplored, and finally emerge successful in my quest for my dream job. If I have to pick one thing—you could call it a trigger—that led me to find a way and take action towards this entire journey, it is my dependence on and faith in self-help books.

Initially, I used to read them, but rarely took any action. Books not only give us the recommended action to achieve something, but also suggestions for ways to change our mindset. Those changes in my mindset started to kick in after I read a few dozen books and followed some influential achievers online.

One such belief that left an impact on me was investing in myself. I completely understood and agreed with the fact that investing in myself is the best investment I could ever make. Instead of buying better cars, houses and various other toys for entertainment, check to see if you can invest in yourself to break your existing barriers in life, such as a nasty job, bad health, broken family relationships, lack of skills or understanding in life. Whatever you feel you are lacking the most is a good point to begin to invest in yourself.

"But where and how do I invest?" you may ask.

There is no dearth of options for this. In fact, you will have more choices that you can use. The world is being transformed into a single capitalistic market where everyone wants sell something. You can find anything for sale, if you know how to Google it. Yes, you can't imagine how much variety is available today for online learning. Go and find out for yourself.

I understood that it requires a lot more work if you really want to get your dream job. You need to assume complete responsibility and become proactive to grab your dream job quickly.

Becoming proactive is about taking control in every stage of finding your job. It's your job and you need to take responsibility, right from understanding *what* you love to do, *where* it is available, *whom* to approach and *how* to get it. You don't want to become confused and blown away by the flood of opportunities thrown at you.

You take control in finding what you love. You approach recruiters in person, instead of just waiting for them to respond. You need to know how to take control in an interview, instead of just answering their questions and waiting for them to decide. You need to know how to take control at the negotiation table. Sending a resume is just a part of finding the job you love, often an insignificant part of it.

There are so many ideas to unpack here and most of them are totally obscure. How do we take control? I have taken each of these ideas and tried multiple approaches to find what works for me.

The idea of taking control is a paradigm shift in my approach to finding my dream job. It puts a lot of responsibility on my shoulders, but also gives me an opportunity to learn this game better. This is a skill of a lifetime. Once you master it, you can apply it again and again, to chase bigger and better jobs.

During the last six years, I spent thousands of dollars on online self-learning courses from some of the most influential people on the planet. After taking a few expensive courses, and reading dozens of books, I found that none of them work for my unique situation unless I try and test those ideas that I learned, in different combinations. I had to customize the methods I learned to make them relevant for exponential technologies.

Learning from multiple books and a handful of great courses online, I customized a path for you to break into exponential technologies.

The DREAM to realize the job you want is also an acronym for the process of getting it. These steps and strategies can give you incredible results, irrespective of your industry and your level in the organizational hierarchy.

Here is the step-by-step process that you can use to reinvent yourself:

D for Discover clears the haze around the abundance of choices in the market. It reveals exciting possibilities that exist outside of your comfort zone, while dispelling the long-held beliefs that made you stay in your dissatisfying job. With this, you can find 2–3 exciting roles that you are sure you can build passion for.

R for Reach guides whom to approach to validate your ideas about your dream job. Those who have traveled the path will open their doors to help you decide if that job is right for you. You'll get clarity like never before and you'll become eager to invest further effort into building the right skills needed to get your dream job.

E for Engage turns you into an expert in the emerging markets. You know where to find the expertise that others envy. This expertise can finally open up the doors to your dream job.

A for Attract takes you to the right job opportunities. You'll know how to prepare your resume just for the job you need, eliminating all the unnecessary clutter in it. It helps you to place yourself ahead of the competition (or even eliminate the crowd altogether), to position yourself as a VIP in front of your potential employer.

M for Master takes you to mastery in the selection process. You will be on a level field with the hiring manager during your interview. It brings the discussion under your control so that you become more confident and even decide the terms of your future engagement. It puts you way ahead of your competition and you become master of the interview and any further negotiation process, ultimately leaving you with a dream job in your hands.

How good is this method?

Well, even I did not know until I met someone after I joined my dream job.

Let's call this person Tom (name changed). Tom was my senior in my earlier company, but I did not know him until I met him in my new company. In fact, when I was in my previous company, I had been dreaming in vain for the position that Tom enjoyed. Finally, I had to resign from there without getting that one promotion. I changed my job and met Tom one day as my colleague in my new company.

Guess what! I found myself in a position where I was senior to Tom in my new company.

Before I could digest that fact, I came to know that Tom did not join this company directly from our previous company.

He went to a prestigious business school for his MBA and got placed in this company directly from the campus. The school Tom went to was ranked in the top 20 in the world rankings for that year. That blew my mind!

In fact, I am not an exception in achieving such an unbelievable result. I know many of my friends and acquaintances have achieved similar results with this approach, so I am sure that you, too, can get your dream job from doing this.

Step 1. D for Discover

The more years of work we add to our resumes, the more restricted we become regarding our future opportunities. Our idea of our self-worth becomes narrowed to the specific industry, business function and even specific capability area we have been working on. It becomes harder and harder to see opportunities that are outside of our limited experience.

We tend to ignore the fact that the key differentiating skill in any job is only a minority in the overall skill set that is required. The majority of the skills needed by most of the jobs are often generic—skills that you might already possess. When you look at the skills that are in the minority (often a technical skill or specialized knowledge), you feel intimidated and do not dare to try for the job. One possible explanation for this is that, the longer it has been since we left college, our interest in learning new skills decreases.

However, it is possible to expose ourselves to new opportunities and become excited about them at any time. With a simple technique called "Window Shopping," I have taken a tour of dozens of industries and hundreds of roles, and revived my professional life.

Let's see how it works.

Window shopping

Just like Amazon brings everything you can potentially buy into a single platform, LinkedIn brought all possible job descriptions into a single platform.

It's humanly not possible to browse all the products on Amazon because it's so vast. Similarly, you can't browse each and every job description on LinkedIn. However, you *can* browse by industry and find the interesting jobs in that industry. Go through these pages like you were window shopping. You don't need to have anything specific in mind, but you may discover new things, and who knows? You may like one or two roles more than your current role.

From the search bar on the LinkedIn homepage, it is a little difficult, but there is a way around it. Use this link to browse different jobs in each industry: https://www.linkedin.com/jobs/directory/ (or Google "Linkedin job directory").

This shows the availability of unique jobs you probably did not know about yet.

Spend a few hours on this site. You know how big the job world is. You will also start to recognize that your existing skills are useful elsewhere, too. Pick out 3-5 job titles that interest you.

For each title, note down the job description. Explore who is doing those jobs in your network and beyond. What does their career growth path look like? What was their previous experience before they took on their current job? Prepare a summary of your observations.

Discover your dream job

There is so much written and said about dream jobs, but in tangible terms, what is it? I am not thinking about a classic, abstract definition, Wikipedia-style.

We all know what it feels like to have a dream job. I wanted to know what essential things I need to know in order to get my dream job. Thankfully, I came to know this from one of the most expensive courses I took on this subject.

A dream job is not about having a specific salary you might have wished for. It's also not about having a perfect working conditions, lots of freebies, etc.

Your dream job is essentially defined by the "Job Role" and the "Company" you aspire to.

That's all you need to nail down. A specific role you want to perform in a specific company defines your dream job. The rest is all add-ons, or even minutiae that you can ignore.

Once I had this clarity, it was so much easier for me to define my dream job. It removed all the confusion in my mind and let me focus on what matters the most.

Using the window shopping technique, explore the job world and make a list of at least 3 to 5 dream roles and your dream companies. This is the starting point for your journey to find your dream job.

Step 2. R for Reach

Our dreams are just a reflection of our inner world. We want our inner world to be reflected in outer reality without making sure that our inner world is a true reflection of outer reality.

Understanding what's possible and how it feels to achieve something, as told to you by someone who has been there and done that, is the only way to break this disconnection between our dreams and reality.

You should validate your dreams before taking any action on them. In fact, the first step towards achieving any goal is to validate if that goal is right for you and decide your priorities based on that finding.

Validate Your Dream Job Ideas

I know you are excited about the job titles you picked up from window shopping. Don't jump into the job portals in search of your dream jobs. You are far from being ready to do that.

What excites you about those job titles may or may not be true in the real world of work. You should validate your excitement before taking any action towards pursuing those career options.

The best way to validate your ideas is to speak to someone who has done that job. Explore your network to see if anyone is already acting in your dream role. You may not find it there. Find those in second-level or even third-level contacts from LinkedIn. I am sure you will find some. Write to them directly or seek an introduction from your existing contacts. Try to meet them in person, if possible. Tell them why you are excited about their job and ask them what they think about your ideas.

Don't become disappointed if what you happen to hear contradicts your assumptions. You will have saved years of unnecessary labor with just one conversation. Learn from the experience and move on to the next job title. You may have to skip over 3 or 5 or even more ideas, before you finally settle on one.

Win Your Inner Battle

Have you ever thought about what stops you from landing your dream job? It's your assumptions. Some are genuine; some are baseless.

We make assumptions when we face conflict between our expectations and reality. Our assumptions may lead to confusion, disappointment, and ultimately inaction.

There is an interesting thing going on here. We often do not consciously know what our assumptions are and, worse yet, we often forget that even with valid assumptions, there are ways to get past them so that we can achieve what we dream about.

When we think of pursuing our career aspirations, we often perceive multiple roadblocks in the form of fears and assumptions that limit us and keep us from making an attempt to achieve our goals. Our assumptions act as mental barriers that keep us from even thinking beyond what we are currently doing.

We are what we think and believe. Based on our belief systems, we make assumptions about our possibilities and life in general, and our beliefs are formed by what we read, experience and observe from our friends and family.

Have you ever thought like this?

1. I am not qualified for that job.
2. I did not graduate from a well-known institution.
3. What if I get that job and don't like it later?
4. Companies don't pay good salaries for my skills.
5. I will not get that job because it is way too many levels above my current job.
6. The market is not good; there are no openings. It's difficult to find job in this market.
7. There are no jobs for my technology/skill set; I cannot change my technology skills at this moment.
8. Changing from a technical role to a management role (or vice versa) is difficult.

Many times, it's not all or even many of these kind of thoughts, but just one or two of them that stop us from taking next step—a step as small as applying for the job we want.

First you need to know what's blocking you, and then you naturally try to find ways to break through the block. Often these mental barriers are so deeply ingrained in us that we generally cannot think beyond our assumptions.

I have numerous examples where people successfully challenged their assumptions and landed jobs that they love. During my search for my dream job, I myself have personally challenged and broken through most of the assumptions mentioned above.

Our assumptions control our life to a large extent, even without our being aware of them. Unless we systematically identify and test them, we will not be able to break through those barriers and think beyond them.

Assumptions are more easily formed when they occur within a community. Your circle of friends and your family play a critical role in forming your assumptions. I have seen people live their entire life, blocked by simple assumptions that many others have easily broken through and achieved their goals early in their careers.

When you look at the jobs you collected from window shopping, what comes to your mind is a list of barriers—your excuses, your assumed inabilities. Some of them may be true and some may be an illusion, but all of them have solutions to enable you to overcome them. At this moment, you probably find that hard to believe.

Start this exercise now.

Use the following table to identify all of your assumptions that stop you from finding and applying for your dream job. Later, I will show you how to systematically de-construct them and find a way to overcome them.

My Dream Job	<<write your dream job here>>				
Key Requirements (from my Dream Job)	My Assumptions (Why I think I am not eligible)	Category (Ex. Experience, Qualifications, Market conditions, etc.)	Challengers (Who overcame these limitations?)	Wisdom to break my assumptions (How did they do it?)

One quick and easy way to find them is by going through the job description for the job you have chosen.

Check each and every requirement and ask yourself, "Why can't I do this job?"

Just write what comes to your mind. At this point, do not concern yourself about whether it is true or false, whether there is a way to solve it or not. Just list everything that says NO to you, everything that keeps you from pursuing your dream job.

You may not find a readily available open position at this moment. The company is not important at this moment. Just take any sample job description that is closest to your dream job. The objective of this exercise is to understand how your assumptions are limiting you and controlling your fate.

Just be honest with yourself when you choose your dream job and list your assumptions about it. You may totally believe that your reason for disqualification due to a particular requirement is true and you cannot change or overcome it in any way, but I still ask you to list them all here.

Categorizing your assumptions would tell you where your greatest fears are. Then move ahead and try to fill up the rest of the table. For filling the fourth column, explore LinkedIn to find people. When you come to the last column, you have to get out of your chair and talk to people to fill out the rest of the table. However, if you can even fill up the table to that last column, I am sure you can find yourself in a better position—one step closer to your dream job.

At the end of this exercise, I am sure you will be surprised to discover what's blocking you. Acknowledging and understanding your fears is the first step in your journey to break through all the barriers that stand between you and your dream job.

Synergistic Networking

One of the dream job principles we learned from the previous chapter is about building the right network. Searching for a job only when you are unemployed or unhappy does not work anymore. You need to generate opportunities all of the time. You need a network that supports you in both a growing or falling job market.

I am sure you already recognize that networking your way to your dream job is far faster and more efficient than you trying to find it by being one in the crowd. However, the challenge that most people face is how to build the network that helps them get what they want. After selecting your dream job, your next step is to build the right network that can help you get your dream job.

You probably think that reaching out to people to ask for favors sounds sleazy. The problem with building a good network is not a lack of moral strength. It is the lack of the right perspective. You want to be friends with someone whom you think might be helpful to you. This simple rule works irrespective of one's social rank, so think of how you *can help* someone before approaching him/her *for help*.

When you try to approach someone way above you in the social hierarchy, the first question that comes to your mind is "How can I help that person?"

You may not be able to help the influential people with your money, personal service, or offering your other network connections. However, you need to accept the fact that influential people also have needs that you can support. They often look for people who can take their advice, implement it and communicate results back to them.

In other words, you can seek a mentor in him or her. Influential people have their mission well defined and they continuously strive to advance their mission. You can take part in their mission and offer your help in advancing *their* mission by taking their words into your network.

This is the way you can build a network that ultimately benefits you far more than what you invested in it. I call this a synergistic network. It should be beneficial to both of you, right from the initial contact.

Yes, it is sleazy to ask others for favors, so don't ask for them. Instead, go to them with a genuine intention to help. I am sure you can build a richer and more fulfilling network this way than simply to try reaching someone and asking for a job in the first interaction. It almost never works.

You need three things to reach practically anyone on this planet.

1. Connect
2. Context
3. Contribution

1. Connect

Find out how you can relate to the person you want to meet. How do you feel when someone far below your social rank approaches you by a cold call or email? Forget about helping; you don't even want to respond to them!

Approaching someone influential with a cold call or email hardly ever works. You need a channel that s/he can relate to. Being part of the same alma mater is one of the best channels to reach people. Otherwise, try to find out if s/he is part of any professional networks that you are also connected to. If you have a common friend, ask for an introduction. If you think a particular connection is really valuable for you and there is no connection available, build your network to establish a good connection before approaching them directly.

2. Context

We are living in the world of an information explosion, such that everyone has to constantly filter for things they want to focus upon. If you think what you are reading now is not interesting to you, you have multiple other things available to entertain yourself.

It's very difficult to catch the attention of someone whom we really want to meet unless we can relate to their interests and their mission in life, so think of the right context before reaching out to someone.

How can you relate to that person so that you can get his/her attention? This context can be sharing his/her mission, values, interests or anything that s/he is currently occupied with. Find common ground.

3. Contribution

When you approach others, especially for help, all that goes on in your mind is about you, you, and you, but unfortunately that does not help you.

You need to practice putting others first when you interact with them, either by email, a direct call or direct interaction. Talk less about you and more about them.

Before meeting influential people, think of everything that you can to be of help to them. Go there to discuss that. Bring him/her the ideas and actions that enable you to help him/her.

You need to practice this to get better at it. It's worth an investment, because there is nothing more important than a synergistic network in order for you to grow in this economy.

Here is what some of my students had to say about synergistic networking:

> "Man, this insight [regarding connect, context and contribution] made me realize how BAD I had become at networking. I made many new connections while applying for an MBA, but after the application process, I stopped contacting those people and didn't even let them know how it turned out. I've gotten to be better at maintaining relationships by using this insight." – Jesse

> "I have a number of people I've always wanted to reach out to but never knew how to do it! I will definitely be using C3 technique with these people.

I HATED networking before this, because it was always a "Snatch & Grab" game of business cards! NO MORE!" — Jeyel

"I've always considered myself to be good at networking, but I've never been strategic in my process. I realize how powerful it can be to meet with the right person. In this case, what you may learn in a thirty-minute meeting with a hiring manager can set you apart from every other candidate." — Jonathan

"There's this belief among people with very good technical skills that if their skills are great, it should do all their work for them. They expect the rest of the world to see how brilliant they are. When it doesn't happen, they blame others, so they tend to be divas and it's very hard to work with them. I've seen this happen a million times. I even used to have the same problem. Lucky me, I figured out that talent is key, but being likable and able to sell yourself is equally important." - Srikanth

People with good ideas and information hang out with one another. The secret to getting something is to follow someone who has already gotten it. But the secret to seeking something from someone is to help him/her before asking anything from them.

Join the relevant communities to help others, before you seek anything for yourself. What specific things do you know or have that the other person does not? Develop skills, interests and experiences in multiple domains, and then act as a bridge for your connections in one circle who want to access the others. If you can do that, you will be seen as immensely helpful.

Step 3. E for Engage

There are no experts today in IoT, AI or in 3D printing, when you consider where these technologies will end up 10 years from now. The capabilities brought by these technologies are greatly desired by almost all of the industries, so the entire world is suddenly trying to embrace them.

The change and improvement in these technologies is unimaginably rapid, so it's almost impossible for any single person to track and master these technologies. This is why you can stand an equal opportunity to become an expert when you compare yourself with other existing experts on these technologies in the market today.

All you need to do is to start engaging with your industry with your ideas. Choose your niche business technology area and follow the market. One way to find your niche is by looking at the cross-section of interesting technology, industry and functional areas.

For example, IoT-based marketing for telecommunications, AI-driven HR for the software industry, etc. Develop your ideology around how you can use these capabilities to transform your niche. To begin with, watch for interesting methodologies, products and solutions that are emerging in other industries and try to apply them to your niche.

Become an Expert

An expert is not necessarily someone who holds a doctorate or who has 20+ years of experience. An expert is someone who knows something that others may not know well.

However small and intricate your chosen niche is, you may find it is already vast and complex. In addition, such a niche area is now vulnerable to the transformative forces of exponential technologies that can continuously create new complexity in your niche. Seeing this, you may become discouraged that you could learn enough to claim expertise in it.

But wait a minute.

Expertise is not eternal. There is a time dimension attached to it. If you received a doctorate in one subject 10 years ago, you can hardly claim expertise in that subject unless you keep pace with it, so you can become an expert at any time if you know how to be on top of things.

In fact, becoming an expert is easier than you think. The easiest and cheapest way is by reading bestselling books on your niche. Go to amazon.com to find the bestselling books on your topic and who the influencers in your industry are. Before buying any book, make sure you read what critics say about those books. After that, buy at least five bestselling books and read them. Check in on your confidence level after that. It should have gone up measurably.

There is also another element to this—learning about something that you may not find in books, such as practical experience, personal stories, etc.

You get it from other people's experiences. Pick three influencers in your niche (or at least those you think have enough experience) and talk to them. Understand how your industry has evolved in the specific niche of your interest and what the critical milestones were. Learn how they solved seemingly impossible problems and overcame major challenges.

That's all you need to do to claim expertise in any area except those that involve manual skills. You can do this comfortably in about three months. If you have done this diligently, you can be one of the top 5% of the people working in your industry when it comes to expertise.

Engage with Your Industry

With the ubiquitous access to quality content and education, it's easy to learn things today. We often forget that it's also equally easy to share our ideas with others. Without spending so much as a single dollar, we can spread our ideas to millions and even billions of people in this hyper-connected world.

You should seriously consider writing your own blog or simply guest posting on leading online platforms. Writing is one of the essential skills of the 21st century. It is also something that computers cannot do as of now. Of course, computers can already analyze and summarize content and present it in multiple other ways, but they are not yet developing new and meaningful ideas.

Try to get your voice out there, through writing, speaking, and contributing to online communities. If you have not written in public media before, practice in online communities by commenting on others' posts, then write your own blog, and then eventually start writing for other influential platforms.

If you have not spoken in public before, the easiest way to start with is by approaching your own school or university. Go there and spend time with the "young guns" who need your advice. Then use that experience to speak at events and training programs at your workplace. Break out slowly into other public speaking avenues, such as industry events and business conferences.

In parallel with doing that, start working on your online profile and presence. It is the only medium through which you can be known to others anywhere on the planet whom you don't know personally. Continuously improve your online profile by engaging with your industry, because it is a proven way to attract the opportunities you most want.

Step 4. A for Attract

Your preparation (the ground work) for your dream job is one part. The other part is finding the opportunities in the job market. In fact, most people only think about the second part without doing any of the ground work I have talked about so far. I can't overemphasize the importance of ground work. I hope you already understand that.

The first thing we think of when we want to find a new job is searching through the job portals. Finding a job from a job portal is like taking an open competitive test for your grad school admission. You are competing with the whole world for a few opportunities. You will find some great opportunities out there, but they will rarely get you what you really want.

Searching for a job is the hardest way to get it. Instead, you should attract the right opportunity by doing all the ground work I talked about. When you have a compelling online profile, are known in your niche market, and have built the right network, you attract the opportunities that are just right for you.

Again, I am not saying you should have a big name and a very strong network. All you need is enough to attract your dream job. Even if you start with zero, you should be able to build your profile and the right network needed to secure your dream job in no more than six months.

When you do your ground work well, you attract the right opportunities by tapping your network. You don't need to go through the painful and unpromising way of finding opportunities from job portals. The ground work is useful not only for attracting your dream job opportunity, but also for performing your job with superior satisfaction and fulfillment.

As entrepreneur Bo Peabody says, "The best way to ensure that lucky things happen is to make sure a lot of things happen."[81]

Make things happen in your synergistic network, and when the time comes, you run into serendipity.

First focus on building your synergistic network and growing it with the sole intention of *contribution* rather than expectation. Only when you see that the other person is ready to help you, even when you don't ask for it, are you then ready to ask for help. Even at that point, I don't suggest you ask for a job opportunity. You should approach an influencer or potential hiring manager for advice on how to find an opportunity or whom to approach. If there is any opportunity with them or even within their network, they will be happy to recommend your profile and you get a VIP pass directly to the interview.

Step 5. M for Master

I was surprised at how naive I had been until I took a course on dream jobs. I used to have a 5-page resume. I did not focus on social skills during my interview. My negotiation skills were almost non-existent. I took whatever was offered to me without further questions.

By taking some of the best courses available in the market and (more importantly) experimenting with the ideas from them, I learned that anyone can become a master of the game of hiring.

While there is so much to learn and practice in order to become a master in this area, I found that the following four principles and my tested strategies to adopt these four principles can take you there.

1. VIP application
2. Pre-connect with the interviewer.
3. Bring a plan.
4. Practice negotiation.

1. VIP application

How often do you prepare a customized resume for a specific role offered by a specific company? We upload our standard resume into a job portal and apply for tens of jobs with the same resume. Of course, we know our success rate from that approach is essentially nil, but we still do the same thing, over and over again. If you are serious about a job opportunity, spend time on crafting your resume just for that job.

For most people, a resume is just a chronological list of their education and experience.

Employers don't care about your history. When they look at your resume, they often find it difficult to single out the right experience they need. They need to extract the right information from your resume, often under severe time constraints, because they need to process dozens of resumes.

The average time a hiring manager spends on a resume is about 10 seconds. If your resume does not catch his/her attention during those 10 seconds, it will end up in the waste basket. So, the next time you write your resume, think of how you can impress your hiring manager in less than 10 seconds.

There is one simple technique to craft your resume for a specific job. Think of what you want to say to your hiring manager first, and then write it in plain English. Keep it as blatantly obvious as possible.

For example, "I am the best person to do this job because I have done _ _ *before and I have* _ _*skills*". After you write everything that you want to convey in plain English, rephrase it into polished language that others want to read. Ensure that each and every word you put in your resume has to earn its place.

With this approach, you will not be able to write more than 2 pages, even if you have 20+ years of experience (including some great success stories) under your belt.

What differentiates you from others is often the cover letter. If you're asked to include a cover letter, make sure that you craft it just for that opportunity. Never send a generic cover letter. It's a sure way to communicate your lack of interest in that specific job. It's also easy to find out whether the cover letter was written or copied from public sources, which would be an even more serious mark against you. You need to demonstrate your interest in that particular job, why it interests you, and why you are the best person to fill it, all in concise and compelling language.

2. Connect with Your Interviewer before the Interview

If you follow the approach I have described to attract your job opportunity, you would already know who your hiring manager is. It's always better to connect with your hiring manager before the interview. If you cannot do that, you can try reaching his/her peers who can influence him/her.

Make sure that you don't ask for a job or any recommendation when you meet with them. Discuss the company goals, strategy, and how they want to deal with their competition. Discuss your aspirations, but *never ever* ask for help. Explore how you can help them in your personal capacity, for example through sharing the quality ideas from what you read, offering your network to extend support, etc.

3. Bring a Plan

Your job interview is not about you. It is about your employer, about how a specific job will be executed, and who can do that well.

You should go to the interview with the intention to discuss what to do and how you can do it better than your hiring manager expects you to do it. Have a clear idea about what to do as part of your job.

Often the hiring manager has no clue how you can deliver the expected results. They only know the desired outcomes, but not really know how to realize them.

Spend a good amount of time to clearly think through these issues and come up with a plan. Write your plan as a brief summary and take that with you. With this, you will make the whole conversation about the job and how you can do it. The interview will no longer be about your *abilities*; rather, it will be about your *plan* to deliver the results they want. This puts you in a totally different league than the other applicants.

The better you do this, the better your chances are for getting hired. This particular insight has dramatically changed my confidence and success rate in interviews.

Hone this skill well before your dream job interview. Practice this technique ahead of time with companies you are not really interested in working for. This technique is going to make you the master of hiring process. You have to take this seriously.

4. Practice Negotiation

The appropriate salary and role gives you respect, access, and authority from your future colleagues. It is an essential component of a dream job.

Negotiating for your salary and whatever else you want (other than salary) is essential, in order to avoid looking for your next job soon after you managed to get this one.

Companies spend a lot of money in hiring and keeping employees. It's not difficult for them to offer 10-20% more than what they initially offered. Don't believe it when they say they don't have a budget. That's a common technique companies use to stop you from negotiating further.

Negotiation is finding the value you can deliver to your future employer and articulating it wisely. Come up with ways how you can add value to the organization and decide where to use those arguments during the negotiation.

The best way to master this skill is through practice.

When I was asked to practice salary negotiation with my friends during one of my trainings, I thought it was a ridiculous idea. After I practiced negotiation with one of my buddies, I realized how effective it was.

Discuss everything that you want to have in your job and have a ready argument for why you qualify for that and how you can bring more value to the company. With skilful negotiation, you can avoid frequent job changes and enjoy your job much more.

A dream job is not something you get by applying for something online and attending an interview. You need to make it happen in your life. It is a mission worth fighting for in any professional's life. It has truly changed both my professional life and personal life. I have seen hundreds of people follow this approach and secure their dream jobs. I am sure it can change your life, too.

Answer the following questions to stimulate your thinking about your own situation:

1. What are your mental barriers that stand between you and your dream job? How do you identify and overcome them?

2. What is the Window Shopping technique? How do you find your dream job using this technique?

3. Do you know what your dream job is in reality? If not, how do you ensure that the job you think you want is actually your dream job?
4. How do you build a synergistic network to grow your career?
5. How do you engage with the industry and build your online presence?
6. What's your current online profile? How do you improve it to attract the right job opportunities?
7. Have you reached your potential recruiters in ways through which they can appreciate your talents?
8. What is the "plain English method"? How do you craft your resume with this technique?
9. What's your master plan to beat the crowd in the interview?
10. Have you mastered the negotiation skills to get what you want from your employer?

The definitive roadmap that is laid out in this chapter is the consistent, comprehensive and reliable way for you to obtain your dream job. There are no shortcuts worth pursuing. What you invest in terms of time, energy and commitment will come back to you many times over if you follow this method thoroughly and conscientiously. It's tempting to skip parts of the process because of the effort required, but stay the course and you will emerge the winner. Given the nature of the race for work during these times, you cannot really afford to do otherwise.

Chapter 14. Living with a Dream Job and Beyond

> *"If you are prepared, and you know what it takes, it's not a risk. You just have to figure out how to get there. There is always a way to get there."* — Mark Cuban

When I secured my dream job, the joy of getting my dream job faded away sooner than I thought it would. Fear of failure started haunting me. I had so many questions in my mind.

1. Do I really know what I am going to do?
2. What if I prove myself as being stupid in front of those people whom I impressed so much in my interviews?
3. Can I become a high performer in the new role? And so on.

I thought I should tackle this problem with a sound strategy and impeccable preparation. I believe in wisdom to solve any problem, so I went to Amazon.com and searched for some bestselling books on this topic. I bought *The First 90 Days*, by Harvard Business School professor Michael Watkins.[82] This book also has an iPhone app that teaches what to do on a daily basis for first 90 days in your new job.

After reading this book, I was a bit relieved. Though I have not followed this book all the way through my first 90 days, I got the message in just the first month itself. I tweaked the principles to suit my situation and added a few things needed for my high-tech job.

Overall, by the end of 90 days in my new office, I had established myself as an expert in Big Data and won the confidence of those who had recruited me. I felt so much more confident about my performance after I had spent first 90 days in my dream job.

Why Only the First 90 days?

The initial days in a new job are critical because small changes in your actions can have a huge impact on long-term results. Executives at all levels are very vulnerable in the first few months in their new job. It is difficult to anticipate the challenges ahead and figure out the ways to overcome them.

Failure to create momentum in the first 90 days can lead to an uphill battle for the rest of your tenure. The first three months are a meaningful and measurable time to prove yourself in the new organization.

You have acquired your dream job, without using any shortcuts or gimmicks. Now you need to learn how to become a top performer at your dream job, and you can do that, too. The following steps can help you succeed.

In order to thrive in the second machine age and especially when you are employed in any of the disruptive technologies, you need to focus on the following five areas.

1. Adapt yourself to the situation.
2. Establish your credibility.
3. Keep learning.
4. Create coalitions.
5. Follow the fundamentals.

1. Adapt yourself to the situation.

Adapting is mentally preparing yourself to move into your new role. For this, you need to put your past behind you and hit the road running. Your earlier skills and accomplishments are not sufficient to make you successful in your new job.

Using your past experience to tackle new problems is like driving a car while only looking at the rear-view mirror. Understand that a new job requires a new approach. If you don't find yourself in a familiar situation, your experience may not help you. Try to understand your situation and avoid unnecessary mistakes. You need to think hard, make conscious decisions and act differently in the new job.

Adapting to unknown situations begins with assessing your vulnerabilities.

Watch out for where you fall short of expectations in the new organization. What is super easy for others in your company that you are uncomfortable in dealing with? It's the culture. It's the way work gets done in your new workplace. This is where you start becoming adapted to the new style of working.

Understanding people and their expectations of you helps you find out where to focus your energies. Your vulnerability in a skills gap comes next. Don't think that you need to be an all-rounder in the area of your expertise.

You only need skills to the extent that your superiors and colleagues expect them from you. In order to identify those expectations and meet them, you need a customized strategy to adapt yourself to your new organization.

Being inflexible is another vulnerability. We get frozen into our habits, opinions, and ways of dealing with a given moment in such a way that we often behave without regard for our fellow human beings.

Becoming inflexible is moving away from reality in order to live within our own inner world. Flexibility is one of the greatest virtues. You need to be aware of your inflexibility more often. When you practice this, you find familiar and friendly places not only at work but also wherever you go in your life.

Match Your Strategy to the Situation

Michael Watkins explains that adapting is aligning yourself to the type of organization you are entering into. The particular business you are going to join can fall into any of the four categories: start-up, turnaround, realignment, and sustaining success.

1. Start-up:

The prevailing mood in start-ups is often one of excited confusion. There is less structure, but more enthusiasm and dynamism. If you end up in a technology start-up, you will find yourself in this dynamic, unstructured environment every day.

You should focus on finding ways to channel that energy into productivity. You need to assemble a diverse set of skills and capabilities, such as people, funding and technology that aims to build new business or get a product or service off the ground quickly.

You need a completely different mindset to thrive in start-ups, especially if you come from a large and mature organization. Adapting to the start-up way of working is essential before you demonstrate any specific skill at work.

2. Turnaround:

You enter into a troubled business, so your mandate is to get it back on track. Similar to start-ups, turnarounds also involve a lot of resource-intensive development work. You may not find the necessary resources such as the right people, technology or processes for you to build upon, so you will have to create them.

Unlike start-ups, the general mood in turnarounds is gloomy and unwelcoming. You need to make tough decisions early on and focus on fresh initiatives to build hope and momentum.

3. Realignment:

You enter into a mediocre business that has high aspirations. You see elaborate processes—plenty of resources here. However, your business is struggling to make progress in the market that is seen in their most successful competitors.

In fact, most businesses fall into this category. There are only a few stars in any industry and also only a few major disasters. The majority of companies find themselves mired in mediocrity. If such a company happens to be your choice of a dream company, you have an enormous mandate to realign its business. For this, you need to focus on redirecting its resources, abandoning ageing product lines and developing new technologies. You also need to focus on realigning the organization's strategy, skills and its culture.

4. Sustaining Success:

You enter into a successful company, which is already one of the leaders in your industry. You are amazed by its strategy, processes and people. You find it hard to differentiate and prove yourself.

Instead, you focus on preserving the vitality of your successful organization and try to take it to the next level. Finding new challenges is highly encouraged in such companies, so you should not miss those opportunities.

2. Establish Your Credibility

You are new to the company, so people don't know about you. Don't assume that people have read your resume. It's not an exaggeration if I say that even your hiring manager might not have read your resume!

People don't get to know about you without your conscious effort. It's your responsibility to let others know about you. And it's a precious opportunity, too, because you can paint a fresh picture of yourself, irrespective of your past.

Promote Yourself

Take responsibility for promoting yourself. Don't think that your work will do that job automatically. It doesn't. People don't have time to review everything you do and appreciate it.

You take control of what you want to bring to the notice of others and especially how you want to put forth your ideas, achievements and future plans. For this, you need to have an idea of what success in your new role looks like and to start creating that picture in your team and with your key stakeholders.

Hit the Ground Running

Companies often delay their hiring decisions until the need becomes urgent. You were hired because your contribution is needed now, so don't expect that as a new hire you have the luxury of spending some time in learning before making a meaningful difference at your workplace.

This is a common mistake that causes people to lose their credibility. You should prepare to hit the ground running from day one. Your bosses, peers, and those to whom you report to directly expect you to be making an impact from the moment they see you at work, so the first 90 days are critical for your success at a new job.

Secure Early Wins

When you come on board, you want your colleagues to feel that something new and good is happening. Early wins not only excite and energize people; they also build your credibility.

Understand your boss's opinion about your accomplishments and his personal priorities in order to plan your quick wins. Also try to make a difference for those whose opinions your boss respects. Depending on your specific situation, make plans to deliver meaningful value as early as possible.

The way you accomplish your goals is also equally important. Your means should not undermine your ends. Ensure that your means are consistent with your organization's culture. The way you create value illustrates the behavior you hope to instill in your new organization. If they are aligned, it's a double win for you.

Early wins are the means to get connected to your new organization. They define the messages you send across about who you are and what you represent, so focus on building your credibility in the first 30 days, and then plan to achieve improvements in performance in the following 60 days.

3. Learn Your Way to Success

The fact that you were offered a job does not mean that you've got what it takes to succeed. It's just that the people who hired you believed in you. You may have the necessary experience, but it can be disastrous to only rely on your experience in a constantly changing environment.

The only way you can succeed in this economy is through continuous learning. It should be part of your "day job". Ensure that you devote time to learning from multiple sources—from books, people, online courses and in-person training programs, etc.

Take Responsibility for Your Learning

Never expect that you will get training for what you need to accomplish at work. It will never happen. Most of the organizational trainings are outdated. The learning and development teams find it hard to keep up with the pace of change in the market.

Also, it's not practical to train each employee with the specific skills needed for his/her job. So when you receive training from your L&D department, it may not work for you as is, without customizing it for your specific needs.

You need to learn from diverse sources, both within and outside of your organization, and to adopt an attitude of experimentation.

Always Keep a List of Things to Learn

Create notes in your notebook or in the note-taking application on your system for your learning agenda. Whenever you encounter any challenge, lack of understanding or clarity about the next steps, make a note about it.

To fill those learning gaps, explore sources from which you can learn. Your list should be clear enough to define your priorities. It should only contain a focused list of questions under a broad topic, so that you can learn an area, but also specifically address your challenges.

Learning from "hard" information, such as financial and operating reports, organization structure, etc. is just one part. In order to make effective decisions, you'll also need "soft" information, such as the organization's strategy, technical capabilities, culture and politics. The only way to obtain this intelligence is by talking to people. Look for genuine sources of information, both internally and externally.

Ask yourself these questions to understand what to learn:

1. What are the biggest challenges you are facing or expect to face at your workplace?
2. Why are you facing these challenges? What should you learn or whom should you consult to solve those problems?
3. Where is the industry going? What are the most promising growth areas that you or your team are not presently focusing on?

You can ask these questions at your team level, department level, and even at your organizational level, if you are ambitious. There is nothing really stopping you from growing if you can manage to learn things along the way.

4. Create Coalitions

Great achievements are possible whenever a group of like-minded people contribute toward a single cause. As an individual, you have a limit on what you can achieve. You can overcome this limit by cooperating with others along your way.

At the workplace, your success depends on the support of people who are outside of your direct line of command. You need to create coalitions across multiple functions in your workplace to accomplish your goals.

Start building your "influence network" that can support your ideas and goals. Find out whom you must influence. Identify early on those who may resist your initiatives and persuade those sitting on the fence to join your side.

Your work may not require you to connect with these people. But sooner or later, you will need the support of people over whom you have no direct authority, so you need to invest time and effort in building your coalitions.

Approach people directly if your work demands it. Otherwise, ask your boss to connect you. Meet as many influencers as possible and try to identify the sources of power in your organization. The usual sources of power are expertise, status in the organizational hierarchy, access to resources, and access to information. However, this may change at times, due to the personality types of the people who hold those respective positions. Your coalition should represent the right mix of people to support you in reaching your goals.

5. Follow the Fundamentals

Always in search of new fads, sometimes we forget the proven and age-old wisdom. I want to remind you of some of the essential elements to succeed in any job. The strategies I outlined above only work when you take care the essentials.

Negotiate Success

If you don't measure what you do, there is no way you can claim success. Many people just play the game, reacting to the situation they are put into, and eventually call themselves a failure because they didn't know what success really is. To avoid this, negotiate with your boss as to what your success really is.

Make it realistic and achievable, because this is your last chance to define your success. If you fail to set the expectations, whatever you achieve may or may not qualify for recognition.

Be Predictable with Your Boss

Nobody likes surprises, pleasant or unpleasant. Yes, even *pleasant* surprises are also a cause for concern for your boss because s/he doesn't have a clue how you made them possible. S/he can attribute the success to luck or help from others or anything else but your own hard work. Stay close to your boss and let him/her know your initiatives, incremental successes and failures. Make sure you clarify mutual expectations early and often. It helps you align the course and reset the goals if needed.

Report Only Those Things That Need the Attention of Your Boss

Don't assume that you only need the help of your boss when you run into problems. In fact, you should take them your problem only if you think it is beyond your control and you definitely need his/her help. If you only approach your boss with problems that makes him/her feel like s/he was the one who is working, not you.

You don't need to review the checklist of all your activities with him/her either. Think twice before you take anything to your boss. You need his/her support in setting the direction and celebrating successes.

Being a top performer in your dream job is as important as getting your dream job in the first place. You can only feel that your new job is indeed a dream job when you enjoy it and realize its promise. You have no choice but to be a top performer at your new job for you to call it a dream job.

Being a top performer is more of mindset than anything to do with your skill set. In fact, when you are working on emerging technologies, there is hardly anything that can be attributed to the skill you brought with you from your past experience. You have to learn every day to remain relevant in the industry and learn your way to continuing successes.

Today, you can learn everything, including how to *find* your dream job and *be successful* at your dream job. You have taken a bold step to learn that from this book. This book is the verbal description of my personal experience and that of hundreds of others whom I know personally. I am sure it can become your story, too, very soon. I wish you all the best in your search for your dream job.

Answer the following questions to stimulate your thinking about your own situation:

1. Do you think you did a great job in impressing your employers that resulted in securing your dream job, but you do not have the necessary skills to perform the job? Deep down within you, do you have that fear of underperformance? Don't worry. Nobody can really escape this fear. Understand the fact that you can learn practically anything and prepare to take on bigger challenges.

2. What are the five strategies you follow to emerge successful at your dream job? Prepare yourself for each of these strategies and apply them at your new workplace.

Conclusion

The world is changing too fast for our genetic make-up. The change is more nonlinear than we think. Because of this, we are increasingly alienated from our environment. We keep finding ourselves in a new world before we become accustomed to the change.

The Big 3 Technologies are taking humanity closer to the technological singularity. Other disruptive technologies are fueling this trend. While these technologies are growing at exponential rates, they are silently triggering automation, also on an exponential scale. Existing occupations are disappearing and new occupations are emerging and they are flourishing unequally, causing envy and inequality.

During the past three years, we saw automation eliminating jobs of varied skills and it's becoming more rampant every day. Every skill that *can* be automated, *will* be automated eventually, and you need to be ready to face this hard reality.

However, the road is not coming to an end. Our innate human qualities (such as creativity and expression) are coming to rescue us because it is difficult for machines to copy them. In the past, every human endeavor that occurred in this world was made possible only by accepting reality and putting one's best foot forward. The threat from automation is not an exception to that. We need to accept today's reality and use our creative juices to race with the machines, in order to thrive in the second machine age. The success from this approach has already been proven in the job market. You will be paid in the future based on how well you work with machines. This is the way to escape automation, and is as real as the threat from automation itself.

An entrepreneur is a truly creative and responsible individual who transcends every possible script that can be automated. To thrive in this economy, every professional needs to acquire the mindset of an entrepreneur. However, not everyone needs to *become* an entrepreneur. In fact, being an *intrapreneur* is a safer option, considering the odds of success for an entrepreneur.

One of the most important skills of the 21st century is techno-literacy. Irrespective of the industry you are in, you have to know the digital technologies. Technology enables you to transcend human limitations and harness the very technology that gave you those powers. Just like driving a 250-horsepower car is like you have the power of 250 horses at your disposal, you will have 250 minds at your disposal with AI in your hand. When you use similar powers from other disruptive technologies, you become more powerful and no individual machine can dominate or usurp your presence at your workplace.

Never before in history has an individual working to earn his/her living had a greater ability to create more money, meaning and freedom than now exists in your imagination. You have the opportunity, right now, to create your future. Go grab it!

* * *

Thank you for reading the book. To get access to all the free resources included with the book (listed below), please visit http://www.bhoopathi.com/r4w

- Just to say thanks for buying my book, I would like to give you the Audiobook version 100% FREE!
- Bhoopathi's 25+ must-read business books to fuel your dream career. (I keep adding more to this list)
- 10 tools and templates to save you hundreds of hours when finding your dream job and being a top performer at your dream job.

- A Ninety-Day goal setting template to translate the book into actionable steps
- Access to a private community to discuss the book and get support from a community of like-minded individuals to inspire, motivate, and assist each other.

Acknowledgements

When I think of the last two years and the way this book took shape in that period, I see my role as being insignificant, when compared with that of all those people who stood behind me in making this book a reality.

I am grateful to Oksana Schippers, who gave me the idea to write this book and encouraged me along the way.

I've had the joy and delight of working with some of my close network on this book. I'm grateful to the early readers who have helped develop the ideas herein:

Entrepreneurs and CEOs who took their time to review my book in spite of their busy schedules – B.V.R. Mohan Reddy, Sukumar Rajagopal, Ankit Jain, Georjios Papadakis, Chaitanya Shravanth, Shantanu Sinha, Ebby Thomas, Ravi Katukam, Praveenkumar A.M., Satyam Bheemarasetti, Anuradha Thota, Suddan Shanmugadasan, Harshavardhan Budaraju, and Prashanth Kasturi.

Industry leaders in large technology organizations who manage multimillion dollar business and/or lead hundreds of people – Deepak Kumar Pelluru, Ravikiran Kakarla, Akshaya Gulhati, Vinay Gupta, Soumyajit Sen, and Amit Tambi.

Shrewd data scientists who can build intelligent machines to relieve humans from work – Sandeep Dulluri, Pavankumar Bandaru, Abraham KP, and Abhishek Singh.

Technology professionals who can assess the impact of automation at their work - Arvind Tiwary, Ajay Ranjit

Vempati, Sumit Roy, Sridhar Raparthi, Visakh Sankar, Akshat Pant, Ravi Pedapati, Parakrama Chandrasekara, Kesavan Hariharasubramanian, and Rajib Layek.

Business professionals who can validate the industry trends using their experience - Patrick Graefe, Vishwanath Machiraju, Ravikiran Motrapu, Somnath Kundu, Prof Sridhar Narayanan, Jean Michel Logan, Suresh Suryadevara, Rajaramesh Chilakala, Raj Elati, Christian Edvinson, Saumar Deka, Bhargav Shelat, Hema Shah, and Nicole Yorke. Thank you all for your invaluable support.

Thank you to the multiple masterminds groups that I have been part of during the course of writing this book. You have pushed me forward to sustain my commitment to complete it.

Thanks to all the writers whose ideas have changed my life and inspired me to transcend my limits: Tim Ferris, Derek Sivers, Tony Robbins, Ramit Sethi, Nassim Taleb, Steven Pressfield, Seneca, Sean Carroll, Daniel Kahneman, Marc Goodman, Jeremy Rifkin, and Peter H. Diamandis, to name just a few.

Thank you to Angie, the cover designer. Thank you Megan for formatting the book.

I extend a huge thanks to Sara Zibrat for her fantastic job editing the book. You really transformed my book.

To Shiri, Aditya and my beloved family: I am forever grateful to be part of my family and for all the love, freedom, encouragement and support I got from you.

About the Author

Bhoopathi Rapolu has spent last five years meeting hundreds of business leaders in multiple industries around the world, helping them to use the emerging disruptive technologies for automation and for their business growth.

Regardless of the industry, country, technology, individual's role, age, or gender, one simple fact stood out: Automation is eliminating jobs like never before, but also opening up some rare career opportunities, again like never before.

Based on his own personal success story in finding his dream job, and hundreds of interactions and dozens of recent books and studies, Bhoopathi wrote *The Race for Work* to provide others with a real-world guide to escape automation, transform their careers, and thrive in the second machine age.

Bhoopathi is an international speaker, author, and blogger. He has published articles on leading international media such as *The Guardian, Financial Times, The Huffington Post, InformationAge,* and *The Times* (UK), etc. Please visit www.bhoopathi.com for more details and additional resources.

Notes (Endnotes)

1. http://www.cisco.com/c/dam/en/us/solutions/collateral/service-provider/mobile-internet/iotwf-whitepaper-realize-promise-iot-revolution.pdf

2. Jim Clifton, The Coming Jobs War (New York: Gallup Press, 2011)

3. https://en.wikipedia.org/wiki/Gross_world_product

4. https://en.wikipedia.org/wiki/World_population

5. http://www.mckinsey.com/business-functions/business-technology/our-insights/four-fundamentals-of-workplace-automation

6. http://www.latimes.com/opinion/op-ed/la-oe-wright-robots-jobs-data-mining-20160328-story.html

7. https://www.weforum.org/press/2016/01/five-million-jobs-by-2020-the-real-challenge-of-the-fourth-industrial-revolution/

8. https://www.cnet.com/uk/news/robots-could-make-half-the-world-unemployed-in-30-years-says-prof/

9. http://www.oxfordmartin.ox.ac.uk/downloads/reports/Citi_GPS_Technology_Work_2.pdf

10. The original tool was built by NPR based on the research finding from Oxford University. You can find NPR tool at:http://www.npr.org/sections/money/2015/05/21/408234543/will-your-job-be-done-by-a-machine

11. http://www.nytimes.com/2012/12/12/opinion/global/jobs-productivity-and-the-great-decoupling.html?_r=0

12 http://www.bloomberg.com/news/articles/2014-04-28/why-factory-jobs-are-shrinking-everywhere

13 http://economictimes.indiatimes.com/tech/ites/infosys-bets-big-on-mana-hires-silicon-valley-talent-to-boost-new-ai-platform/articleshow/52722527.cms

14 http://economictimes.indiatimes.com/tech/ites/infosys-bets-big-on-mana-hires-silicon-valley-talent-to-boost-new-ai-platform/articleshow/52722527.cms

15 http://tech.economictimes.indiatimes.com/news/corporate/tech-mahindra-wants-to-automate-it/53516118

16 http://kpcbweb2.s3.amazonaws.com/files/90/Internet_Trends_2015.pdf?1432738078

17 http://www.forbes.com/sites/bernardmarr/2016/09/23/how-machine-learning-big-data-and-ai-are-changing-healthcare-forever/#405efb534f49

18 http://www.kurzweilai.net/machine-learning-rivals-human-skills-in-cancer-detection

19 https://hbr.org/2016/03/3d-printing-is-already-changing-health-care

20 http://futurism.com/artificially-intelligent-lawyer-ross-hired-first-official-law-firm/

21 Peter Diamandis and Steven Kotler (February 21, 2012). Abundance: The Future Is Better Than You Think. Free Press, Tantor Media.

22 http://www.theguardian.com/society/2015/oct/05/world-bank-extreme-poverty-to-fall-below-10-of-world-population-for-first-time

http://ourworldindata.org/data/growth-and-distribution-of-prosperity/world-poverty/

23 https://ourworldindata.org/world-poverty/

24 https://en.wikipedia.org/wiki/Decline_of_newspapers

25 http://www.nytimes.com/2011/11/07/opinion/krugman-here-comes-solar-energy.html?_r=1&hp

26 http://www.pewglobal.org/2015/07/08/a-global-middle-class-is-more-promise-than-reality/

27 https://en.wikipedia.org/wiki/Joseph_Schumpeter

28 http://www.forbes.com/sites/tomiogeron/2013/01/23/airbnb-and-the-unstoppable-rise-of-the-share-economy/#11d1487e6790

29 Jeremy Rifkin (April 1, 2014). The Zero Marginal Cost Society: The Internet of Things, the Collaborative Commons, and the Eclipse of Capitalism. Kindle Edition.

30 http://www.e4s.co.uk/part-time-jobs/how-to-sell-photographs-online.htm

31 https://www.pwc.com/us/en/technology/publications/assets/pwc-consumer-intelligence-series-the-sharing-economy.pdf

32 http://www.industryweek.com/blog/how-will-internet-things-help-manufacturing

33 http://www.ibisworld.com/industry/global/global-car-automobile-sales.html

34 http://www.abundantsolar.com/

35 http://www2.deloitte.com/content/dam/Deloitte/ca/Documents/insights-and-issues/ca-en-insights-issues-disruptive-manufacturing.pdf

36 https://en.wikipedia.org/wiki/Mandatory_renewable_energy_target

37 http://www.nrel.gov/tech_deployment/state_local_governments/basics_value-of-solar_tariffs.html

231

38 https://solarpowerrocks.com/arizona-solar-power/solar-panels-from-the-electric-company/

39 http://www.themanufacturer.com/uk-manufacturing-statistics/

40 http://www.theguardian.com/books/2012/may/24/self-published-author-earnings

41 Taylor Pearson, 2015. The End of Jobs: Money, Meaning and Freedom Without the 9-to-5. (p.118) Kindle edition on www.amazon.com.

42 https://www.pwc.com/gx/en/managing-tomorrows-people/future-of-work/assets/reshaping-the-workplace.pdf

43 http://themisescircle.org/features/files/2013/04/world-economic-history-587x310.png

44 Tim Ferris (April 24, 2007). The 4-Hour Workweek: Escape 9-5, Live Anywhere, and Join the New Rich. Kindle edition on www.amazon.com.

45 https://en.wikipedia.org/wiki/World_economy#/media/File:World_GDP_per_capita_1500_to_2003.png

46 http://www.dailygalaxy.com/my_weblog/2009/09/a-singular-something-in-sixty-years.html

47 http://www.reuters.com/article/us-tech-ai-conference-idUSKCN0YP035

48 http://www.forbes.com/sites/miguelhelft/2016/04/28/in-annual-letter-sundar-pichai-says-computing-and-google-will-be-driven-by-artificial-intelligence/#1260cebf3b84

49 https://www.marketingweek.com/2016/05/18/how-brands-are-using-artificial-intelligence-to-enhance-customer-experience/

50 http://www.wsj.com/articles/if-your-teacher-sounds-like-a-robot-you-might-be-on-to-something-1462546621

51 https://www.wired.com/2014/10/future-of-artificial-intelligence/

52 https://www.eurekalert.org/pub_releases/2016-05/imi-dla052416.php

53 http://news.mit.edu/2016/artificial-intelligence-produces-realistic-sounds-0613

54 http://www.techinsider.io/teslas-autopilot-reduces-accidents-2016-4

55 http://www.deccanchronicle.com/technology/in-other-news/010316/self-driving-car-indian-techie-builds-autonomous-tata-nano.html

56 https://techcrunch.com/2016/05/17/otto-founded-by-ex-googlers-is-bringing-self-driving-technology-to-trucks/

57 http://newsroom.ucla.edu/releases/microscope-uses-artificial-intelligence-to-find-cancer-cells-more-efficiently

58 http://arstechnica.co.uk/the-multiverse/2016/06/sunspring-movie-watch-written-by-ai-details-interview/

59 http://www.theverge.com/2016/6/1/11829678/google-magenta-melody-art-generative-artificial-intelligence

60 http://www.lawgazette.co.uk/law/artificial-intelligence-mimics-judicial-reasoning/5056017.fullarticle

61 http://www.recode.net/2016/6/6/11863534/slack-artificial-intelligence-AI-noah-weiss

62 http://www3.weforum.org/docs/WEF_GAC15_Technological_Tipping_Points_report_2015.pdf

63 http://www.voanews.com/content/netherlands-implements-internet-things-network/3400551.html

64 http://www.pwc.com/us/en/industrial-products/publications/assets/pwc-next-manufacturing-3d-printing-comes-of-age.pdf

65   https://3dprint.com/49489/boeing-3d-print/

66   http://3dprintingindustry.com/news/dubai-unveils-3d-printed-office-80043/

67   http://www.forbes.com/sites/aarontilley/2016/06/02/ibm-cisco-watson-internet-of-things/#24f12bab564a

68   https://techcrunch.com/2016/05/10/3dprintler-lets-you-order-a-3d-print-via-chatbot/

69   Thomas Davenport.and Julia Kirby (30th June 2016). Only Humans Need Apply - Winners and Losers in the Age of Smart Machines. Published by Harper Collins

70   http://www.csail.mit.edu/System_predicts_85_percent_of_cyber_attacks_using_input_from_human_experts%20

71   Kevin Kelly, "Better than human: Why Robots will—and must—Take Our Jobs," *Wired*, December 24, 2012.

72   Erik Brynjolfsson and Andrew Mcafee. (18th February, 2014). The Second Machine Age: Work, Progress, and Prosperity in a Time of Brilliant Technologies. Kindle edition on www.amazon.com.

73   https://hbr.org/2012/10/data-scientist-the-sexiest-job-of-the-21st-century/

74   http://www.wired.co.uk/article/brain-power

75   http://www.cio.com/article/3072132/it-skills-training/10-most-in-demand-internet-of-things-skills.html

76   http://www.theatlantic.com/technology/archive/2015/06/the-internet-of-things-you-dont-really-need/396485/

77   http://www.flowofhistory.com/units/west/11/FC74

78   Tom Rath. (1st February, 2007). Strengths Finder2.0 published by Gallup Press

79 https://www.ted.com/playlists/171/the_most_popular_talks_of_all

80 Duncan Mathison and Martha I. Finney (20th September, 2009). Kindle edition on www.amazon.com.

81 Bo Peabody, Lucy or Smart?: Secrets to an Entrepreneurial Life (New York: Random House, 2004).

82 Michael D. Watkins, The First 90 Days: Critical Success Strategies for New Leaders at All Levels (23rd April, 2013) Kindle edition on www.amazon.com

Made in the USA
San Bernardino, CA
17 January 2018